GW00721805

how to be a
better....

interviewer

THE INDUSTRIAL SOCIETY

The Industrial Society stands for changing people's lives. In nearly 80 years of business, the Society has a unique record of transforming organisations by unlocking the potential of their people, bringing unswerving commitment to best practice and tempered by a mission to listen and learn from experience.

The Industrial Society's clear vision of ethics, excellence and learning at work has never been more important. Over 10,000 organisations, including most of the companies that are household names, benefit from corporate Society membership.

The Society works with these and non-member organisations, in a variety of ways – consultancy, management and skills training, in-house and public courses, information services and multi-media publishing. All this with the single vision – to unlock the potential of people and organisations by promoting ethical standards, excellence and learning at work.

If you would like to know more about the Industrial Society please contact us.

The Industrial Society
48 Bryanston Square
London
W1H 7LN
Telephone 0171 262 2401

The Industrial Society is a Registered Charity No. 290003.

how to be a better....
interviewer

Margaret Dale

KOGAN
PAGE

The
Industrial
Society

YOURS TO HAVE AND TO HOLD

BUT NOT TO COPY

The publication you are reading is protected by copyright law. This means that the publisher could take you and your employer to court and claim heavy legal damages if you make unauthorised photocopies from these pages. Photocopying copyright material without permission is no different from stealing a magazine from a newsagent, only it doesn't seem like theft.

The Copyright Licensing Agency (CLA) is an organisation which issues licences to bring photocopying within the law. It has designed licensing services to cover all kinds of special needs in business, education and government.

If you take photocopies from books, magazines and periodicals at work your employer should be licensed with CLA. Make sure you are protected by a photocopying licence.

The Copyright Licensing Agency Limited, 90 Tottenham Court Road, London, W1P 0LP. Tel: 0171 436 5931. Fax: 0171 436 3986.

First published in 1996

Apart from any fair dealing for the purposes of research or private study, or criticism or review, as permitted under the Copyright, Designs and Patents Act, 1988, this publication may only be reproduced, stored or transmitted, in any form or by any means, with the prior permission in writing of the publishers, or in the case of reprographic reproduction in accordance with the terms and licences issued by the CLA. Enquiries concerning reproduction outside those terms should be sent to the publishers at the under-mentioned address:

Kogan Page Limited
120 Pentonville Road
London N1 9JN

© Margaret Dale, 1996

British Library Cataloguing in Publication Data

A CIP record for this book is available from the British Library.

ISBN 0 7494 1902 4

Typeset by DP Photosetting, Aylesbury, Bucks
Printed and bound in Great Britain by
Clays Ltd, St Ives plc

CONTENTS

ACKNOWLEDGEMENTS

My thanks go to Jane and Steve for kindly reading and commenting on the proof as both job hunters and interviewers and as ever, for ever, to Roger.

HOW TO BE A BETTER... SERIES

Whether you are in a management position or aspiring to one, you are no doubt aware of the increasing need for self-improvement across a wide range of skills.

In recognition of this and sharing their commitment to management development at all levels, Kogan Page and the Industrial Society have joined forces to publish the How to be a Better... series.

Designed specifically with your needs in mind, the series covers all the core skills you need to make your mark as a high-performing and effective manager.

Enhanced by mini case studies and step-by-step guidance, the books in the series are written by acknowledged experts who impart their advice in a particular way which encourages effective action.

Now you can bring your management skills up to scratch *and* give your career prospects a boost with the How to be a Better... series!

Titles available are:
How to be Better at Giving Presentations
How to be a Better Problem Solver
How to be a Better Interviewer
How to be a Better Teambuilder
How to be Better at Motivating People
How to be a Better Decision Maker

Forthcoming titles are:
How to be a Better Negotiator
How to be a Better Project Manager
How to be a Better Creative Thinker
How to be a Better Communicator

Available from all good booksellers. For further information on the series, please contact:
Kogan Page
120 Pentonville Road
London N1 9JN
Tel: 0171 278 0433
Fax: 0171 837 6348

1

INTRODUCTION

WHAT IS AN INTERVIEW?

An interview is a social encounter between two or more individuals with words as the main medium of exchange. It is a peculiar form of conversation in which the ritual of turn-taking is more formalised than in the commoner and more informal encounters of everyday life.

Farr (1984)

The interview is an important means of gathering data about one individual by another (or others). It provides the vehicle which allows one individual to express views and opinions to others in structured ways. The kinds of interviews we experience in everyday life range from the ones seen on TV, to the market social research interview, to job-based interviews, which include appraisal, disciplinary and, most commonly, the selection interview.

Recent surveys conducted by recruitment consultants and the personnel press indicate that over 95 per cent of jobs are filled following an interview. Generally, an individual applying for a job is met formally by the representative of the employer who may be accompanied by others from the organisation. The applicant is asked questions and may be given the opportunity to enquire about the job and the employing organisation. Despite its popularity, a typical one-to-one interview is known to be a poor predictor of subsequent performance in the job. Research carried out over a number of years demonstrates that other techniques achieve better results. Nevertheless, many managers and experienced recruitment professionals remain loyal to the interview, believing it to be a valid predictor of the candidate's subsequent performance. We can only assume that there is something about the interview that needs to be recognised and valued. Rather than convince managers to abandon their tried and tested practices, this book is intended to provide practical guidance to help improve on the current situation.

The general term 'interview' tends to imply that there is only one form. This is not so; there are several ways and different times in the appointment process when a variation in technique can be effectively used. I will explore the most common types and when these are best used, as well as discuss who should be involved and the preparations they and others should make, good preparation being the key. If you see the recruitment and selection process as a continuous flow which needs to be designed and planned, then the interview can be considered as one of the components.

Even when careful preparations have been made, the way in which the interview is conducted may destroy the best laid plans. If constructed well, an interview can be transformed from a gentle ramble around the candidates' prior employment and life history, or a falsely pressurised grilling, into a purposeful interchange. If the person leading the interview is aware of the potential pitfalls and errors that can be made when making decisions, many of the common mistakes can be avoided. Once the 'best' candidate has been selected and offered the job, how they are treated after the interview stage can have an effect on their lasting impression of the organisation and the likelihood of their accepting an offer of employment.

Interviews can be gruelling experiences for both managers and candidates. This book is intended to help managers improve the interview's effectiveness and make the process less stressful for all the people concerned. It provides guidance, tips and examples for managers to follow and, for candidates, insight into what goes on from the employer's perspective. This, I hope, will help with preparations and reduce some of the uncertainty, especially if it is your first interview. Before looking at the process in detail, we will consider why the interview is still the most favoured way of appointing applicants.

WHY INTERVIEW?

Not many people admit to enjoying job interviews, so why do we continue to do it to ourselves and others? Surveys have repeatedly shown that interviews are the most common means of appointing people into jobs, yet research into the effectiveness of selection techniques demonstrates that the typical interview is generally a poor predictor of subsequent success in the post. Impressions such as those given in Figure 1 make it difficult to defend the typical one-to-one interview.

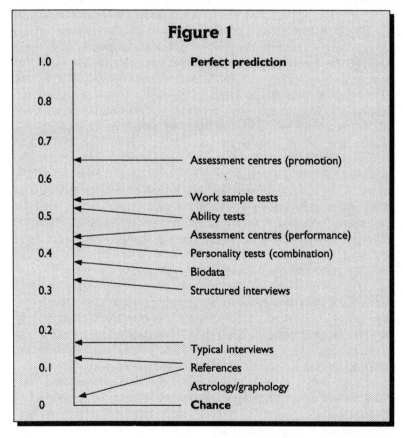

Figure 1

1.0	**Perfect prediction**
0.8	
0.7	
	Assessment centres (promotion)
0.6	
	Work sample tests
0.5	Ability tests
	Assessment centres (performance)
0.4	Personality tests (combination)
	Biodata
0.3	Structured interviews
0.2	
	Typical interviews
0.1	References
	Astrology/graphology
0	**Chance**

From Smith, Gregg and Andrews, 1989

Anecdotal evidence supports the figure:

These contrived situations are not even a reliable test of self confidence. I once interviewed a hopeful whose qualifications were exemplary. Much of what she said at our meeting was drowned by the nervous rattle of her coffee cup and saucer. The confident fellow we appointed proved to be self-infatuated rather than self-assured and was unable to get on with his colleagues. And he couldn't do the job.

(Richard Stanley, The Times, 24 August 1995)

We can approach the decision to employ someone as we would an investment in a major piece of equipment. For example, would you decide to buy a new car on the basis of a half-hour chat on the garage forecourt, a brief inspection of the car's outside and a look through the handbook? Yet frequently, we decide the best candidate on the basis of a brief letter of application and CV, one meeting and, perhaps, a letter of reference from an unknown third party. The cost of employing an individual on an average salary for a year amounts to about the same as buying a good-quality car. Most employees stay in a job longer than most owners keep their cars and the running costs of a car are normally a lot less. Employees cost their employer more than just their salary. They use stationery, make phone calls, need a desk and office space and create work for others. All of these must be included when calculating the size of the investment. The total bill soon shows why it is worth making the effort to get it right first time.

Getting the right person into the right job is a key part of any manager's role. With most managers depending on the work of others for their success, many of us know (sometimes from bitter experience) how difficult it is to put right an appointment mistake. It can also be costly and time consuming to sort out a bad appointment which can lead to all sorts of operational problems, causing wastage, lost production, damage to team work and ruined customer relations. It is far better and, in the long run, more cost effective to make sure the right person is appointed in the first place.

As Smith, Gregg and Andrews showed, the more modern techniques, such as assessment centres, work samples and tests, are known to have better predictive capabilities. Graphology is commonly used in Europe and psychometric instruments have increased dramatically in popularity in the UK over recent years. *The Times* article goes on to say:

> There is no fool-proof way of predicting ability. The most reliable method is probably one involving psychometric assessment, graphology, project work and IQ tests. An interview to make sure. But until companies feel the need to quadruple their recruitment budgets, the interview lottery will continue.

If these other methods are known to be so much more superior, why does the lottery continue? Why do we cling to tradition and continue to make the mistakes which are so well known and well reported in personnel and management text books? The answer to this is really quite simple.

REASONS FOR INTERVIEWING

On the surface the interview has one main purpose: it provides the meeting place where the manager can pose questions directly to each candidate for a job and explore, face to face, with them the relevancy of their knowledge and experience.

It is the chance to 'test the cut of their jib' and see if they are up to the job. Many managers believe that meeting candidates in this way is the only way to test their abilities and personal qualities.

There are in fact four other functions an interview can perform.

1. Managers can judge whether the candidates are likely to fit in with existing staff, the team and the organisation's values. Most managers want to see what the candidates look like and find out if they like what they see. Many believe they can tell the best candidate from the early stages of the interview. The strength of the handshake, whether the candidate waits to be asked or sits down straight away, making eye contact are all common indicators used by managers to decide which candidate will perform the job the best. We will discuss later why factors such as these provide more scope for error than accuracy in decision making.

2. Managers want to see candidates to assess their potential for future performance. It is not easy to understand how, in practice, a discussion is able to achieve this latter purpose, but many managers believe they can recognise the qualities of a future star.

    Consequently, most of the interview should be designed to explore the individual's background and their experiences. Wicks (1984) says 'the majority of job interviews employ this (biography) approach, often, however, in an undisciplined fashion, hunting and pecking at a person's history. The candidates are expected to demonstrate their abilities and form a good impression. They are under scrutiny and assessment.'

3. Generally, little consideration is given to the needs of the candidates. Yet they, too, are in search of the information they need to enable them to judge if the job is right for them. They will have questions to ask about the role, its component tasks, the conditions of employment and the organisation. But, there is a huge power gap between the employer and the potential employee in the interview setting.

    The employer can ask almost anything of the candidate. Probing the accuracy of the information given as part of the application; challenging the candidate to test their levels of assertiveness and putting individuals 'through the mill' to check their ability to withstand pressure are comparatively normal ploys used by managers. Moreover, even though some questions (such as childcare arrangements) are discriminatory unless they can be demonstrated to be related to the needs of the job and posed to every candidate equally, it takes a brave candidate to refuse to answer a dubious question.

    Convention limits candidates' questions to bland and 'safe' topics. Questions about salary, development opportunities or relocation allowances are normal. Questions about an employer's health and safety prosecution record are not often expected and are perhaps not the sort of question a potential employee should ask. Similarly, a candidate refusing to answer or asking why a particular question has been posed is more likely to be seen as indicative of a potentially trouble-some employee rather than one who is concerned and interested in the process.

4. The fourth and perhaps most important reason is to allow the employer and candidates to meet each other. Peter Herriot (1989), one of the UK's leading researchers and author on recruitment and selection methods, has long claimed that despite the technique's poor record of predicting subsequent performance in the job, the interview has a valid place in any appointment procedure. To improve prediction, he argues, the interview should be supplemented with other methods rather than replaced. The interview's purpose is to provide a forum for exchange.

The obvious exchange is that of information – the employer wants to know about the candidate and the candidate wants to know about the employer. The decision to offer a job and the decision to accept that offer bring the employer and the employee together as parties in a legally binding contract. They both require information to form that contact. Additionally, the contract of employment places different obligations, rights and responsibilities on both parties and so the interests of both deserve due consideration in the formulation of the terms and conditions.

The second exchange is more of a social nature. The face-to-face meeting of potential employee and potential employer allows both parties to assess whether they believe they will like each other enough to form a mutually beneficial contract and working relationship. After all we spend, on average, in excess of 7 hours a day, 5 days a week for 48 weeks of the year at work. The exchange of personal information, establishment of rapport and the two-way assessment of 'fit' are the vital first stages in the building of a long-term relationship.

Some argue that a single meeting should not be the only basis from which the parties make the decision to enter into a contract and begin a relationship that may last several years. Most marriages have a courtship and business partnerships are established after a period of negotiation regarding terms and conditions. Why should an employment decision worth several thousands of pounds be taken after only a 45-minute, one-sided discussion. Other selection techniques have been increasingly used in the 1990s, each claiming to have better success in predicting subsequent performance in the job. They provide different ways of gathering information from and supplying it to candidates. However, we can only make passing reference to them here. They are described in full in Dale (1995) (see References list). The criticisms levelled at the modest interview has meant that it has experienced some recent neglect in the standard texts.

The value of the interview is recognised by writers other than Herriot. Bassett (1994) argues that the interview has possibly received bad press because it was 'not properly studied or because it is complex in ways that make it difficult to control and measure'. He cites some recent research that suggests the technique can claim better predictive validity than that previously described, because of improvements made to the training of interviewers.

It is possible to offer managers some very real hope of being able to make valid selection decisions using the familiar technique which, with only some minor modifications, will be able to withstand criticism. The required improvements can be put into effect comparatively easily. Additionally, the interview can be used in different ways at different points of the selection process, giving real opportunities for potential colleagues, peers and others who will work with the newly appointed employee to meet, question each other and exchange opinions.

Remembering that the core purpose of the interview is to enable a manager and candidate to find out whether they will be able to build a mutually satisfactory relationship.

The manager needs to know the answer to the following questions:

❑ Will I be able to work with this person?
❑ Are they the best person for the job?
❑ Will they work well with the rest of the team?

The candidate equally needs the answers to the questions:

❏ Will this job provide me with the outcomes I want from employment?
❏ Will I be able to work productively for this manager?
❏ Will I get on with the other members of the team?

In our enthusiasm to improve the interview, we must recognise its limitations. The interview does not examine the candidates' abilities to do anything else apart from answer verbal questions and present themselves in a contrived situation. What it does allow is the opportunity for candidates to explain their approaches to work, their history, and what they are likely to do in given situations. Additionally it provides (or it should do) the chance for candidates to ask questions they might have about the job, the circumstances surrounding it, the employer and conditions of employment. If the employer needs to test other skills alternative ways of assessing an individual's abilities are required.

WHAT IS TO COME

Even though I have implied that there is only one type of interview, most people know of the one-to-one and panel interviews; these are only two of the many other possible forms of interview described further in Chapter 2.

By taking some simple steps you can avoid some common slip ups, for example the wrong candidate turning up at the wrong time in the wrong place, or a key interviewer not turning up at all. Spending a little time planning what information needs to be exchanged at which stage of the process also ensures that everyone knows what is happening so reducing the chance of mistakes. There are times when special or different treatment should be given to particular individuals. These are outlined in Chapter 3.

How an interview is conducted also has a marked influence on its effectiveness. The reason for the exchange is two-fold:

1. to satisfy the employer's need to gain enough information about a candidate so that a prediction can be made about the individual's likely performance in the job; and

2. to enable the candidate to find out whether the job will provide for their desired outcomes.

How to organise and conduct an interview is covered in Chapter 4, and Chapter 5 describes some of the errors that are made when taking decisions following the interview. These are made by both parties, and constitute the biggest problem in the process, for these errors are common and occur frequently when one person makes subjective judgements about another. While the errors are inherent, steps can be taken to reduce their impact.

The final chapter explores what happens after the interview has been concluded; the events following the appointment and how the early stages of the relationship between the employer and employee will influence the success of the appointment.

It is good practice to offer feedback to both successful and unsuccessful candidates. They deserve more than just the interview experience in return for the time and effort they spent in submitting their applications. Feedback to candidates needs to be handled with care as it can have legal implications, so I will suggest some dos and do nots of the post-interview period. Similarly, managers should also consider seeking feedback from candidates. All concerned can improve their performance, given constructive comments.

As this book is concerned with improving the effectiveness of interviewing for the benefit of the interviewers, those being interviewed and the organisation that employs both, examples of good practice will be given to provide guidance. Checklists and tips support the narrative and advise managers on what action can be taken, easily and practically, to improve their interviewing technique.

I also hope to help the individual attending an interview by providing insight into the interview process 'from the other side'. This will assist the candidate to prepare, and therefore make the most of the opportunity.

Many of you reading this will have substantial experience of being interviewed and conducting interviews. You will have your own views on what works and what doesn't, what can help and what can hinder. The purpose of this book is to provide some alternative suggestions; try them out, see if they work, gather feedback, reflect on the data and then decide whether your practice has improved and talk to your colleagues about your approaches. We can always make improvements, and exchanging experiences and learning from other practitioners is one way of developing our practice.

Interviewing done well takes time and effort but, considering the size of investment being made, the possible effect on the lives of individuals, success of managers and the effectiveness of organisations, continuous improvement will pay back and make becoming a better interviewer a worthwhile achievement.

2

CHOOSING THE RIGHT INTERVIEW

INTRODUCTION

Recruitment and selection are normally described as a single process made up of separate stages:

1. Advertise
2. Recruit potential candidates
3. Answer queries and provide more information
4. Screen applications
5. Shortlist applicants
6. Interview candidates
7. Appoint

This simple picture severely limits the contribution the interview can make to the desired outcome. As there are several different types of interview and difference occasions when the interview can be used, the decisions about when to use the interview and which form it is to take should be made when designing the overall process. This should be planned at the outset to ensure that the information needed by both parties for their decision making is gathered and supplied effectively.

Example 1

High-Tec Finishes wished to employ an engineer with highly specific knowledge of surface coating materials. The Projects Manager knew that it would be difficult to judge the extent of technical knowledge from application letters and CVs. Consequently it was agreed that the candidates with the required qualifications and experience would be asked to attend a preliminary interview. Based on this and the other information supplied by the candidates, a shortlist would be drawn up and the individuals asked to meet the appointment panel.

Example 2

When the marketing assistant left, the PR Manager decided that it was essential to appoint a new person who would complement the remaining team members, and that the team felt comfortable with the appointment. He decided that the suitably qualified candidates would be invited to meet the team to discuss their perceptions of the job and the organisation. He also felt that it was important for the candidates to talk to existing members of staff about their preferred working practices, priorities and approaches. The PR Manager wanted to be confident that the new employee would share the organisation's values on professional practice, customer care and confidentiality. Following the discussions, the team would agree the final shortlist and the candidates would be clear about what would be expected from them.

The one-to-one and panel interview are the most commonly used, although their known flaws have led to widespread criticisms. Chapter 1 outlined some reasons why the interview should be improved rather than rejected and replaced. The face-to-face interview permits the employer to assess the candidates, and the candidates are able to question the employer. Moreover, it enables both to assess their fit with each other. Both the candidates and the employer will need, at some point, to discuss their separate expectations and be sure they will be able to reach a shared understanding of what the job will mean in practice before they enter into a binding legal agreement. There can be no doubt that there is a real need to enhance the interview's ability to predict performance and improve its standing. This can be achieved by using the right form of interview at the right time and by involving the right people.

Improvements can be made easily by training interviewers, improving the design of the process and making more informed choices about when to use which type of interview. This chapter explores the options and the variations that can be made to the face-to-face interview.

WHY USE ANOTHER TYPE OF INTERVIEW?

It may seem that introducing more stages just drags out the time needed to fill the vacancy and makes it unnecessarily complex. But remembering that the decision to employ an individual, even on a part-time or temporary basis, can be paralleled to the purchase of a piece of expensive equipment, the assessment of candidates' match against the requirements of the job and the candidates' assessment of the suitability of the employer can be seen in a different way. Additionally, employment law is designed to protect individuals against employers who believe there is nothing wrong in simply sacking bad appointment decisions. It is better to take a week or two longer and introduce several structured opportunities to exchange and check information, rather than just relying on one brief interview at the end of a process.

Interviews for the preliminary exchange of information

The first chance an employer has to come into contact personally with prospective candidates is when they seek information about a vacancy. Frequently this contact is made over the telephone, in the form of informal discussions or via a recruitment pack. The latter tends to be the preserve of large employers who have both the resources and the numbers of vacancies to justify the expenditure.

Sometimes it is more economical and more effective to organise an opportunity for prospective employer and potential employee to meet face to face. This meeting allows candidates the chance to find out more about the job and organisation directly from someone 'in the know'. It also gives them the chance to ask questions as well as providing the employer with the opportunity to make some initial judgements about the individuals.

Example 3

Home Stores is a national chain of DIY shops whose distinctive feature is the provision of expert advice to amateurs. When the company decided to open another branch in a market town it decided to adopt a novel recruitment strategy as the locality had a high level of unemployment and its traditional skill base was neither building nor retailing. About 80 staff would be needed, ranging from joiners, plumbers, painters, to act as technical advisers, sales staff, office and managerial staff.

The company's personnel staff organised an open day in a local hotel. Videos showing another of the company's stores were run and existing staff from other branches were brought in to answer questions. These staff also carried out initial skill assessments of the members of the public who expressed a firm interest in the jobs. The initial assessments took the form of 'technical' interviews. The interviews for the people wanting to be Advisors were designed to explore the extent of their knowledge. They also permitted some assessment of their interpersonal skills and abilities to answer questions clearly. Those applying for the sales jobs were asked to complete numeracy tests and to take part in a short role play with an 'angry' customer. After the role play they discussed, in small groups led by an experienced salesperson, how they dealt with the situation. Applicants for the clerical and managerial positions were asked to take appropriate aptitude tests and to participate in an interview designed to explore their attitudes to work and their understanding of support roles.

Continued on next page

Continued from previous page

On the basis of the interviews and test results, Home Stores contacted a number of individuals after the open day and invited them to submit formal applications outlining their relevant paid and unpaid experience. The individuals' skill and experience profiles were then considered in comparison with the 'ideal profile'. This thorough approach had been designed to recognise that while many people in the town had limited relevant or recent work experience, they may possess the skills the company was seeking. It also gave the individuals an opportunity to see what the company was offering and to talk to existing employees – potential peers – about the company as an employer. It also promoted Home Stores as an organisation that was considerate and professional.

Similar interviews to the one described in Example 3 are used by large employers. It tends to be most cost effective when large numbers of individuals are needed or when a lot of applicants are expected. For example, many employers, usually the larger companies, use preliminary interviews when directly recruiting graduates. The university and other centres of education organise a 'fair' or 'milkround'. Employers set out their stalls which are frequently staffed by recruitment specialists. This approach is particularly worthwhile when employers are in competition with each other for the best graduates.

Preliminary interviews can remove the need for long applications and the problems these can cause for shortlisters. However, they can also reduce line managers' involvement in the selection of their own staff. This can be dangerous as it could provide managers with an excuse if the individual appointed is less than ideal. This is not a valid argument – how many managers are in the fortunate position of being able to appoint all their staff? Most find they are obliged to manage staff appointed by their predecessor. In any case the management of performance is a clear managerial responsibility, regardless of who appointed the individual. This danger can be overcome if a team working approach is taken that ensures the proper and timely involvement of line managers. For example, managers could (and should) participate in the specification and revision of appointment criteria.

Interviews to screen applications

While the preliminary interview allows pre-application meetings, screening interviews take place after an individual has become a firm applicant. The employer checks an individual against the job requirements by comparing the applicant's CV or application against predetermined criteria. The long-listed individuals are then invited to attend a screening interview which is conducted by line managers and personnel specialists or, if they have been used, by search or recruitment consultants.

Various instruments can be used to aid the screening interview. Some employers and consultants make use of psychometric, aptitude or cognitive ability tests at this stage; others use structured interviews. Sometimes the candidate can be asked to attended several meetings. In some organisations, it is normal for candidates for senior professional posts to visit the organisation to meet key individuals. These are likely to be those with whom the future employee will need to develop close working relationships such as potential peers, managers, staff, clients and other colleagues. The meetings will also be with the key decision makers. Typically most of these meetings take the form of unstructured discussions and any assessment of candidates is carried out the basis of impression and discussion rather than firm evidence of the ability to do the job (see Example 4). Makin (1989) suggests some ways in which selection for professionals may be improved. These include the use of cognitive tests, personality tests, work samples and educational attainment.

Example 4

The position of Chief Pathologist had attracted a lot of interest. This level of post in a leading teaching hospital did not occur very often. The Trust's Chief Executive decided to shortlist in the traditional way and then invite the candidates to meet, informally, a number of key individuals. The Head of Human Resources arranged a series of group meetings over a three-day period with several of the surgical consultants, members of the department, the management team of the Trust and teaching staff from the local university's Department of Pathology. Each group was asked to plan their own slot with the candidates and to involve other people they thought would be most appropriate.

At the end of the three days, representatives selected from each group met to decide who should proceed to formal interviews. The meeting was lengthy and highly charged. Each group had used its own criteria to assess the candidates. Not everyone had made notes and one representative could not remember which candidate was which. Eventually the Chief Executive closed the debate and decided, for herself albeit, on the basis of what had been said about each, which candidates should attend the final interviews.

Not every screening interview needs to be like this. They can be improved significantly by planning and organising structured meetings which also provide the candidates with the opportunity to meet key individuals and see the organisation from various aspects. The employer also obtains the information it requires from the candidates. This is achieved by designing a process which permits a thorough exploration of the candidates' abilities to do the job against laid down, agreed and understood criteria.

The types of structured meetings include:

❑ A question and answer interview with each group being allocated specific areas to cover. This is similar to a focused discussion group. Alternatively this type of meeting can take the form of sequential interviewing (see below).

❑ A structured interview can be held after a series of tests such as cognitive ability or aptitude tests, a work sample or case study. In the case of the latter the interview would explore how the candidates approached the task, why they made certain decisions or chose courses of action and what conclusions they reached. Examination of experience, other skills and areas of knowledge would take place at another time, and the candidates would be given other opportunities to obtain the information they required.

❏ A structured interview, organised so that the questions posed to the candidates explore the criteria and aspects relevant to the job in question and each candidate is asked the same questions in the same way. Various examples of the different forms of structured interview, such as situational and behaviour event, will be given later.

The use of a common assessment form provides a consistency between the groups, improves note keeping, facilitates the reporting of the assessments and forms the basis of needed records.

Final interviews

The final interview should be the last formal meeting to be held between the candidates and the employer before the decision is made regarding the offer of employment. This interview can be conducted by one individual representing the employer or, in some extreme cases, by a committee of over ten members. Neither of these is a good predictor of performance and each is prone to the pitfalls well known to occupational psychologists but less well reported in personnel management text books. These include relying on first impressions, using stereotypes, making cause and effect judgements on limited evidence and the halo effect (see Chapter 5 for a fuller explanation of these).

TYPES OF INTERVIEW

As well as choosing when to use an interview, different forms can be used to elicit different types of information from candidates. In this section we will discuss four forms – the one to one, panel interviews, small groups and sequential interviews. All of these can be used as vehicles for the preliminary exchange of information, to screen candidates or as the final meeting leading to the decision to appoint.

One-to-one interviews

The one-to-one interview is usually conducted by a representative of the employing organisation. This individual will be authorised to meet candidates to obtain and provide information about a particular job or a range of job opportunities. Sometimes this form of interview is structured, sometimes unstructured. A structured interview, described below, ensures that each candidate is asked exactly the same questions in a similar fashion. This is to ensure equity of treatment and to make sure that all required areas are adequately explored. An unstructured interview allows the interviewer to follow up on interesting answers, and probe areas depending on how the candidate responds to the questions and situation. It is possible to use both structured and unstructured questions.

The one-to-one interview can be made to be a highly stressed occasion. The justification for this is to explore how the candidates respond to pressure. Some organisations prefer to make the interview more relaxed, believing it is easier to get candidates to be open and honest in this sort of climate.

Some argue that the one-to-one interview gives the greatest opportunity for the interviewer and interviewee to establish 'rapport'. It is also claimed that it is easier for the interviewee to relate to one person at a time. This point may be valid for some forms of interview, such as giving feedback, performance appraisal, counselling, or investigation, but in the context of forming a contract of employment, the degree of rapport and ease of relating should be minor considerations. The most important factors are the giving and gathering of sufficient and good-quality information on which the employer is able to base a prediction of performance, the candidate is able to assess whether the job is likely to provide the desired outcomes and both are able to make an informed decision.

The one-to-one interview has a low co-efficient of predictive validity, despite its popularity. Its main weaknesses lie in how we all make subjective judgements of others and form decisions based on these 'flawed' conclusions. These will be discussed in Chapter 5. The one-to-one can be improved if more people are involved and its structure designed. Some of the methods given below will suggest how these improvements can be made. The interview can also be combined with some other means of obtaining information from and providing it to candidates. These can include tests, work samples, problems to be solved and the candidate's findings discussed.

Panel interviews

Some people may think that panel interviews are time consuming and intimidating to candidates. Typically a candidate is interviewed by between two and twenty people. Large committee interviewing is not very effective nor a particularly satisfactory way of exchanging information. A reasonably sized panel of between three and six people can be an effective decision-making body providing it is well structured, organised and run properly.

Example 5

The Sales Manager needed another salesrep to join the Northern team. Being involved in the appointment process, she decided, would present a development opportunity for the team's administrator. It was company policy that a member of the personnel department supplied information about the contract, conditions of employment and organisational features as well as being an independent assessor. She also wanted to involve a member of the sales team, as she thought it would be useful for them to tell the candidates what working for the company was really like. The team member would also carry out the 'expert' assessment of the candidates' sales skills and knowledge. With the manager, the panel would consist of four people, each with their own distinctive contribution to make to the process.

Continued on next page

> *Continued from previous page*
> The members of the panel were called to a pre-interview meeting to plan the organisation and structure of the interview. The manager wanted to make sure that each member of the panel knew why they had been asked to participate and what role they would occupy. She also wanted them to be clear about how the interview would be conducted. The tone of the interview was agreed, the order of questioning, the way candidates would be welcomed and what would be said to them as they left were agreed. Each member of the panel worked out how they would explore their allocated areas and rehearsed the wording of each question with the other panel members to ensure that the questions were unambiguous. Then, together, they double checked against the person specification to make sure that every criteria would be covered. Finally they discussed how the final decision would be made and feedback offered to the candidates.

Small groups

Small groups of interviewers can be used to conduct in-depth or technical discussions with candidates. They also provide a means of involving staff and key others in the process without giving them direct influence on the appointment decision. In particular using small groups allows the interview to:

❏ *Focus on a particular aspect of the job* and involve 'experts' as interviewers whose role is to test the degree of each candidate's technical knowledge.
❏ *Be advisory.* Key individuals – social leaders, experts, representatives of customers – can make recommendations to the decision makers and suggest which areas of performance, knowledge or experience are in need of further exploration at subsequent interviews.
❏ *Be mainly social.* The prime purpose would be to ensure 'social fit' by exposing future colleagues to each other early in the process.
❏ *Be political,* allowing key individuals to believe they have a more influential role in selection decisions than they really have.

❏ *Contribute to the decision-making process.* Representatives of each small group can report their findings to and/or participate in the final appointment panel.

The value of small-group interviews is not given as much credit as it deserves. This is partly due to its image of wishy-washy liberalism and pseudo-democracy, and partly because it is seen as time consuming. In fact, the cumulation of people's views, gathered in a systematic and proper way, can contribute enormously to decision making, especially if the appointee is to work closely with others internally or with customers and suppliers. To make best use of the small groups, they need to be planned and the role of the participants must be made explicit to all involved, including the candidates.

Example 6

Trentbridge Housing Association wanted to be sure that the new area manager would receive the support of the existing staff and residents. The post had become vacant after a series of problems: the previous manager had been found guilty of fraud and theft, and had, over a period of some months, duped residents and bullied staff. His crimes had only come to light after a routine internal audit examination found some irregularities and an investigation started. Most staff and residents had been afraid, even then, to speak openly.

As this climate of fear and suspicion remained, the management of Trentbridge was very anxious to build high degrees of involvement into every stage of filling the post. They decided on a staged selection process that would involve the candidates in several meetings with key individuals from the area.

It was agreed that the appointment panel would be composed of the Operations Manager, a representative from the Housing Association's personnel function, a senior member of staff from the area, a representative from the Tenants' Association and an advisor from one of the Association's other area offices. Their first task was to agree the job requirements and person specification.

Continued on next page

Continued from previous page

The 26 applications received in response to the advertisement were compared against the job requirements and person specification. The 11 long-listed candidates were then invited to visit the area, see some properties, meet staff and residents and attend a preliminary screening interview with the advisor, another representative of the Tenants' Association and senior member of staff. This interview was designed to explore the candidates' understanding of housing legislation, the issues facing tenants and their vision of the future. The questions were factual and interviews structured. On the basis of the candidates' applications and the findings of the preliminary screening interview, the long-list was reduced to six.

The remaining candidates were invited to participate in a selection process leading up to the final interviews. The process comprised a series of meetings with three small groups. The first was a group of tenants who concentrated their questioning on the way in which the area manager could influence the tenants' quality of life. Before the interview the group (five tenants chosen by the Association to represent the full area) met to decide the indicators they would be seeking. Drawn from the job requirements and person specification, they included how the manager would create systems for the open discussion of problems, the establishment of a code of conduct for staff, how 'problem' tenants would be dealt with and what sort of community activities could be initiated. The second group of five staff, ranging from the latest recruit to the most senior, would focus their questioning on matters relating to team building, the code of conduct, development of skills, and communications systems. The overlaps were deliberately constructed to allow for cross-checking later. The third group was a management group whose purpose was to check on approaches to management and provide the candidates with the opportunities to get answers to some of their questions.

After the interviews a 'rapporteur' from each group met with the Operations Manager and personnel specialist to report and combine their assessments. Each group had used a form which contained the relevant criteria and a rating scale so that assessments could be easily amalgamated. On the basis of the evidence and assessments, the results of the earlier interviews and the candidates' application forms, the Area Manager and personnel specialist decided which of the candidates should meet the appointment panel.

The main argument against using small groups is the negative effect of group dynamics. Lack of management and clear definition results in confused agendas and people having different expectations. These lead to disagreement about the process rather than concentrating on gathering evidence and making assessments of the candidates. Moreover, and sometimes inevitably in organisations, internal politics spread from one area of work to another and unduly influence the interview. However, these dynamics can be managed to ensure they do not detract from the interview's primary purpose.

The fear of this sort of situation happening is used as a reason for not involving people in interviews, but, if involved appropriately, they can make a very valuable contribution to the process. To maximise involvement, the dynamics of groups need to be recognised as normal parts of human behaviour, and the steps that can reduce the negative impact identified. For example:

❑ Make sure that all members of the group understand their role and its limits (for example, they are advising the selectors, not making the appointment decision; they can recommend areas for further exploration, not reject candidates).
❑ Make it clear where the group interview fits into the overall selection process so that group members can see how their contribution complements other stages.
❑ Make sure that all members of the group understand the job requirements, the person specification and the criteria being used.
❑ Rehearse the part each group member is to play in the interview, including the phrasing and sequence of questions, timing and how the assessment against the criteria is to be made.
❑ Train group members in the skills of observing and listening, note taking and making assessments against criteria.

Sequential interviews

Sequential interviews are very similar to small-group interviews. Several interviews are held, one following the other, and each is conducted by one person who explores a particular aspect, such as experience, technical knowledge, managerial approaches, attitudes to quality etc.

Example 7

A company wanted to appoint a new training executive. The short-listed candidates were invited to a selection event during which they met each of the three selectors separately. Following this they were asked to make a presentation to the three together and then participate in a final interview.

Each of the three selectors had their own area of interest for exploration with the candidates. The first was the Personnel Manager who wanted to be sure that the person appointed knew how to, and would be able to, develop the function to a level beyond its current administrative role. The second was an operations manager who wanted to integrate training into a major change programme currently being planned. The third was a branch official from the Trade Union. This official was also a representative on the Regional TUC Education and Training Sub-committee and extremely knowledgeable about both the latest government initiatives and the availability of grant aid. She also wanted to explore with candidates how company training priorities may be linked to personal development programmes for her members.

The questions each interviewer were to pose had been agreed before hand and structured so as to explore the requirements of the job. These had been put into a *pro forma* for each interviewer to complete for each candidate. These would be used later when the final decision to appoint would be made. The presentation was designed to explore the professional skills of the trainer. The topic had been chosen so the candidates could outline the career development steps of a training officer to allow their understanding of the role to be checked. A similar form was used by the three interviewers. At the final interview panel, they explored the candidates' fit with the organisation and gave them the chance to discuss the company and ask questions about the job.

Sequential interviews contain all the weaknesses of one-to-one interviews. They do allow for mechanisms to be built in that can reduce their negative effects, for example:

❑ The use of pre-determined criteria.
❑ Choose the interviewers carefully on the basis of their contribution to the process.
❑ Make sure each understands their role and its limits.
❑ Plan the areas that each interviewer will cover in relation to the overall selection process.
❑ Use a *pro forma* to record observations against the criteria.
❑ Combine assessments after the interviews and other phases of the selection process.
❑ Train the interviewers.

INTERVIEW DESIGN

As with any managerial task, an interview can be purposefully designed to achieve certain ends. Effective design means being clear from the start what you want to achieve. For example the main aims could be one or all of the following:

❑ The exchange of information to predict the likelihood of candidates being able to perform to the standard required.
❑ The provision of information needed by candidates so they can decide whether the job will provide them with their desired outcomes.
❑ To enable everyone concerned to reach their final decisions.

Depending on the choice of aim, a process can be constructed with operating parameters set out.

There are five main types of interview:

1. The **structured interview** generates information in response to specific questions. It is good for testing knowledge and facts.
2. The **situational interview** gets candidates to imagine themselves in hypothetical situations and answer the question 'what would you do if...?'. It is good for assessing how candidates may behave in future similar situations.

3. The **oral examination** explores how the candidates have responded to a case study or approached a piece of work. It is good for assessing how candidates behave in a given situation.
4. The **criterion-based interview** directly addresses areas of knowledge, skills and abilities specifically required for the job. It is good for exploring attributes and abilities in a tightly focused way.
5. The **behavioural event interview** examines, in detail, the candidates' past performance to explore their abilities. People's past behaviour patterns tend to be good predictors of future behaviour as people, generally, are consistent.

Structured interviews

Recent research suggests that structuring interviews – ensuring that each candidate is asked exactly the same questions in the same way – can raise the predictive validity of the interview. It can be very tight, examining the candidates precisely using closed questions, or it can be loose but still structured, with questions constructed to allow the candidates to discuss the same topics but giving scope for follow-up questions and in-depth probing. The reason for designing an interview with an underpinning structure is to ensure that all the criteria are examined and that the candidates are treated in the same manner.

The steps to take to construct a structured interview are:

1. Carry out a job analysis to identify the knowledge, skills and abilities required for effective performance.
2. Rank these in terms of comparative importance and contribution to doing the job to the standard required.
3. Draw on 'experts' (ie people who are specialists or knowledgeable about the area of work) to help with the construction of the questions, so the questions explore the required areas.
4. Test the questions on people who hold similar jobs to the one vacant (make sure they are performing to the desired standard). Check for clarity of phrasing, answerability and appropriate level.

Depending on the circumstances, it may be desirable to give the candidates the questions before the interview. They can be sent out with the invitation to attend the interview. Alternatively the candidates could be given them just before they join the interviewers.

It is better if more than one person conducts a structured interview. Having at least three interviewers allows one person to ask the question, one to observe, the other to make notes. The fourth, if there is one, can be listening and considering any supplementary or follow-up questions.

Using a rating scale improves the quality of the observation and recording as it focuses the interviewers' attention. The interviewers need to be trained in its use and should rehearse rating interviewees' responses. This preparation can be done at the same time as testing the questions.

Example 8

Help Yourself Stores required another security operative. The Branch Manager prioritised the following outcomes:

❑ High match between the number of people questioned, and those proven to have been engaged in shoplifting.
❑ High degree of acceptability to shoppers.
❑ High levels of conviction of people caught shoplifting.

To achieve these, the person appointed would need:

❑ to be able to make accurate observations and interpretations of shoppers' behaviour
❑ well-developed interpersonal skills
❑ an acceptable appearance
❑ to be able to question tactfully and thoroughly
❑ to be able to compile accurate and detailed written reports.

The manager asked the company's Head of Security to help with the questions, which were then tested by a panel of three interviewers brought in from other branches. A checklist was used by the

Continued on next page

Continued from previous page

interviewers for recording their observations of the candidates against the criteria. The rating scale ensured consistency and simplified reporting the assessments to the manager.

The candidates were told before the interview that there would be two parts. The first would be very structured to probe their knowledge and skills, while the second would be less formal and would be designed to allow the interviewers and candidates to discuss the job and explore how each would match the other.

Situational interviews

A situational interview is one in which candidates are asked the question 'What would you do if...?'. The 'if' could be a situation that might arise in that job; even if it is an artificial scenario it needs to be based on a possible event.

Example 9

Each candidate for the post of Security Operative was asked to describe how they would, if appointed to the post, deal with the following situation:

'You saw a member of staff handling a colleague's handbag. The same day the second individual reported to you that a large sum of money was missing from her purse. What would you do?'

Alternatively the situation can be generated by conducting a critical-incident analysis of an event that actually occurred and, using the elements, construct the situation for the candidates to address.

Example 10

Candidates for the post of administrator were each asked:

'Despite having planned the meeting, booked the room and ordered refreshments in plenty of time, you arrive to find the room is not prepared and there is no sign of the coffee. What reasonable steps could you take to make sure that this sort of situation does not occur again?'

Another way to prepare a situational interview is to 'crystal-ball gaze' by looking ahead at a hypothetical event that might happen.

Example 11

The candidates for the post of Production Manger were asked:

The company has well-established quality-control and assurance systems which rely on clearly defined sampling criteria and laid-down procedures. The company is proud of its record and ensures strict adherence to BS5750. The criteria were established as a result of statistical analysis, and on the basis of many years' experience, are known to be reliable. The last quarter's returns have shown a degree of variance well outside the confidence limits. Internal investigations have shown that the procedures were followed correctly and no unusual incidents occurred to explain the poor quality of the goods produced.

Being responsible for quality, what steps would you take to find an explanation for the variations, and to prevent their re-occurrence?

Situational or hypothetical interviews can be very useful in finding out whether the candidates are able to think themselves into the job, provide practical solutions to problems and respond quickly. The interview can take the form of a discussion or a question and answer session. Alternatively, give the situation to the candidates before the interview and ask them to produce a written report or make a presentation outlining their proposed actions.

In preparing the interview, it is worth testing the situation on someone with a similar background, experience and knowledge expected of the successful candidate to make sure that:

❑ The situation is realistic.
❑ The question is capable of being answered under the false conditions of a job interview in front of a panel of 'experts'.
❑ The knowledge needed to answer the question is likely to be possessed by each of the candidates equally; any specialist knowledge required to answer the question is generally available among suitably qualified individuals, not just existing employees, which would disadvantage external candidates, or is of a technical nature that any competent professional would know.
❑ The phrasing of the situation is unambiguous.

Oral examination or presentation of the results of a piece of work

The candidates can be given a case study or 'problem' to work on, either when they arrive for the interview or sent to them in advance. In either case, the candidates should be told that they will be expected to complete a piece of work and will be asked questions about it as part of the interview.

There are arguments for and against giving candidates the case or problem in advance of the interview day:

❑ Not all candidates will have the same amount of time available, due to pressures of their current job, domestic situation or simply the inefficiency of the postal system.
❑ Some candidates may be able to access facilities and other resources which will give them undue advantage when preparing their answers.
❑ Some candidates may be able to enlist the help of others and so it may not be clear to the interviewers whose work is being examined.

❑ Some candidates may misinterpret the brief and, not being able to check, may waste a lot of time answering – brilliantly – the wrong question. This may not be the fault of the individual – the question may have been unclear in the first place.

Giving the case or problem to the candidates when they arrive may not allow them to demonstrate fully their abilities. The falseness of the situation, the pressure, and the unavailability of resources and information may inhibit the candidates unduly. It also means that they cannot take the time to think, reflect and research in a way that would normally be part of dealing with a situation at work. The unseen case or problem may be an effective means of exploring what an individual is able to do alone, but it does not allow for any assessment of the candidates' abilities to work as part of a team.

Criterion-based interviews

A criterion-based interview is concerned solely with the exploration of the knowledge, skills and abilities required by the 'ideal' job holder. These will have been identified during the job analysis as essential for the effective performance of the job. Even if a detailed job description has not been compiled, a role outline can be the basis for a person specification.

Example 12

Trainee Accountant

Role purpose

To provide professional accounting support and advice to line managers as a member of the management information and accounts team.

Key duties

1. To produce periodically financial, written and verbal reports, using computer databases and other sources of information.

Continued on next page

Continued from previous page

2. To explain to line managers any variation from budget and highlight other areas in need of attention.
3. To recommend action to redress significant variations and capitalise on positive trends.
4. To participate in and contribute to internal training programmes.

Person specification

Knowledge

1. Accounting conventions.
2. Budget management techniques including standard costing and variance analysis.

Skills

1. Computer literate.
2. Compilation of accurate financial reports.
3. Preparation of concise and clear written reports.
4. Ability to give clear verbal presentations.

Abilities

1. Influencing skills.
2. Analysis and solving of problems.
3. Interpersonal and team-working skills.

The criteria listed in the person specification are expanded to aid the assessment of the candidate's behaviour.

Example 13

Analysis and solving of problems

Being able to:

❏ Diagnose problems in complex situations based on the analysis of available data.
❏ Make sensible assumptions to cover gaps in data.
❏ Propose workable solutions individually and as a member of a group.

From these statements, a series of questions for use during the interview are generated. Unlike the situational interview which explores responses to and behaviours shown under certain conditions, the questions used in criterion-based interview directly address the sought for features and aspects of behaviour expected from the ideal candidate. The questions are usually based on actual parts of the job or ask the candidates to describe, in detail, their own skill levels.

Example 14

Sample questions for Trainee Accountant

❑ Tell me how you would produce a quarterly financial analysis?
❑ What sort of indicators would you look for to tell you if a budget was running to target?
❑ Would you use any data other than that produced from the accounts? Give examples.
❑ What would you do about missing data?
❑ If you found a major variation, what would you do?
❑ What are important features of being an effective team member?

The criterion-based interview allows the interviewers to focus precisely on the areas they wish to explore and gives the opportunity to probe each in some depth. This needs sensitive application, or the candidates could leave feeling as though they have been subjected to a grilling. It is better if the questions are put in the form of discussion topics, rather than the blunt examples given above. For example, 'Let's talk about producing financial reports. How would you go about it?' is likely to get more from the candidates than 'How do you produce a financial report?'. The phrasing of questions will be discussed later.

Behavioural event interviews

Behavioural event interviewing was developed initially as a means of gathering data to distinguish between an average performer and a superior performer. Since then the technique has been extended to cover job interviews. The same fundamental design principles are used to discover what an individual is capable of doing. This is done by using their past record as a means of predicting what they are likely to be able to do in the future. The following principles underpin a behavioural event interview:

❏ The interview is structured (each candidate is asked the same questions and treated in the same manner).

❏ The questions focus on the candidates' past behaviour. Past behaviour is a reliable indicator of future action and patterns of well-established behaviour are likely to be repeated in the future. This does not deny the individual's capacity to learn and change: unless an intervention is made, conditions surrounding the individual remain constant and there is no reason for change, an individual's behaviour tends to remain stable.

❏ The questions explore the most, least, hardest, easiest, and so on, type of situations the individual has faced.

Example 15

If the job requires the appointee to make sales presentations, the question could be:

'Tell me about the most difficult presentation you made:

❏ What was it about?
❏ How did you prepare?
❏ What made it hard?
❏ What did you do about it?
❏ How did you make the presentation?
❏ What was the result?

If you had to do it again, how would you do it differently?'

❏ Follow-up questions are prepared to enable the interviewers to probe further, if required.

❏ The candidates are rated against job-related criteria, which are behaviourally specific, using a rating scale.

❑ The candidates are not compared, at this stage, against each other nor are their personalities assessed.

If the technique is to obtain its full effect, and be applied properly, you need to take the following steps:

Analyse the job by identifying what the postholder will be expected to do. This is done by specifying the key tasks and result areas through the compilation of a role outline or job description and a person specification. Ways of carrying out this analysis include:

❑ Interviewing the previous postholder.
❑ Observing what those doing similar jobs do in practice.
❑ Asking customers of the postholder's products to describe the products and services they expect.
❑ Asking the manager what a successful postholder will be doing in a year's time.
❑ Predicting likely difficult situations that will need to be tackled by the postholder.

Identify the key behaviours required for effective performance in terms of knowledge, skills and abilities by testing each major area of activity against the following questions:

❑ What does the postholder need to know to be able to perform above average?
❑ How would I know an above average performer when I saw one?

Construct an appropriate rating scale. Each area of knowledge, skill or ability should be rated on the same general scale, for example:

1 = unacceptable
2 = nearly adequate
3 = adequate
4 = above average
5 = good
6 = excellent

Alternatively each criterion will have its own ranking with its own descriptor and ranked behavioural statements on a unique rating scale, as Example 16 illustrates:

Example 16

Communication
Ability to express ideas and convey information clearly and concisely using appropriate media, checking to make sure the messages have been understood.

Rank	Definition
1	Makes no effort to communicate.
2	Misleads or confuses.
3	Understood with difficulty.
4	Understandable, but not concise.
5	Communication is initiated. Is clear and concise. Some checking of understanding.
6	Communication is initiated. Is clear and concise. Checks understanding and takes action to clarify any misunderstanding.

Design questions and probes which will enable the criteria to be explored from the candidates' past experience, and examine their knowledge and skills.

Example 17

Tell me about a time when you wrote a substantial report and presented it to an audience.

❑ How did you structure the report?
❑ How did you present it?
❑ What reaction did you get?

Test the questions to ensure they are unambiguous and answerable. This may be done by posing the questions to a sample group of existing employees who are at the standard of performance that the postholder will be expected to attain. However, take care candidates do not get to hear about the questions before the interview.

Train the interviewers to pose the questions and use the rating scales. All the interviewers need to develop a shared understanding of the criteria and the meaning of the behavioural statements.

Ask the interviewers to answer the questions themselves to give 'a taste of their own medicine'. Sometimes, interviewers fail to appreciate how difficult a seemingly easy question can be to answer under the pressure of an interview. This is also a good way of checking that the questions are clear and are likely to give the sort of evidence being sort.

The interviewers need to practice using the rating scales as, at the end of each interview, they will be asked to rate the candidate and make adequate notes to enable them to give their reasons for the rating. A typical *pro forma* used for this purpose is given in Example 18.

Example 18

Candidate ....

Criteria	Question	Rating	Evidence
Communication Ability to express ideas and convey information clearly and concisely using appropriate media, checking to make sure the messages have been understood.	Tell me about the time you wrote a substantial report and presented it to an audience?		

Continued on next page

Continued from previous page

Criteria	Question	Rating	Evidence
Problem solver Ability to diagnose and solve problems in complex and ambiguous situations.	Describe the last time you recognised a problem in an organisation in which you were involved.		
Computer literate Knowledge and ability to use computer software commonly found in offices to an elementary standard.	Which software programmes have you used? What main benefits did they have for the work you were doing.		
Group worker Ability to work productively with several people on a joint task.	Tell me about a team project you have been involved in at school, work or in your social life. What role did you play and what was your main contribution?		

Pool the ratings given to each candidate after they have all been seen and produce a summary report. This is then given to the decision makers to help them decide who to see at the final interview. The reports can also be used as a basis for feedback to the candidates, should they choose to receive any, or to inform the initial training plan for the person appointed to the job.

The behavioural event interview does not make the decision.

Like all other forms of data collection, it merely provides information and evidence to enable the people involved to make their judgements.

Dos and don'ts

❏ Plan and prepare the whole process before starting to fill the vacancy.
❏ Decide what skills, knowledge, abilities and experience are being sought and how best to obtain the evidence needed to demonstrate their existence.
❏ Decide how many stages need to be built into the selection process and when an interview would be an appropriate selection technique to use to gather information from candidates and supply them with the sort of information they need.
❏ Decide which sort of interview to use to obtain the information you need.
❏ Consider what the candidates will want to know at which stage of the process and how best to transmit that to them.

Consideration also needs to be given to:

❏ who will design the interview
❏ who will conduct it
❏ what training and other support will be required
❏ who is available to supply any help needed
❏ how to assess after the event; were the interviews held at the right time? Did the form make a positive contribution to the cost effectiveness of the appointment?

The next chapter will provide some answers to these and advise on the preparations needed.

3

Preparing to Interview

'Proper planning prevents poor performance'

Even appointing a temporary, junior member of staff can be equated to an investment decision worth several thousands of pounds. The importance of getting the right person is illustrated when you consider the effect of a poor switchboard operator on the quality of the organisation's customer service. Most investment decisions are made on the basis of informed choice. Normally time and energy are expended to ensure that adequate information is obtained and all available options considered. The same principles apply when appointing staff: taking similar steps can help to reduce the chances of making a poor appointment.

The main purpose of an interview is to enable the exchange of information so that both parties are able to make the decisions they think will maximise their chance of getting their desired outcome. In this chapter we explore what information is needed, what preparations need to be taken to ensure that it is obtained efficiently and effectively, and how best to make use of it. We also consider what special arrangements may be required by members of disadvantaged groups. The roots of discrimination lie in prejudgements. Consequently, we briefly explore the nature of stereotypes and erroneous assumptions in order to account for the way in which they distort assessment and decision making in interviews.

WHAT INFORMATION IS NEEDED?

Even before applications have been received by the employer, some information about the job and organisation will have been provided to potential candidates. (Ways of doing this have been described in Dale, 1995.) When preparing for an interview, take account of what has and what has not been sent out already. The amount of information will depend on the sort of recruitment medium used and whether candidates have been asked to complete lengthy application forms, send in CVs or submit brief letters. Regardless of what has been sent out, early impressions of the employer will have begun to be formed in the minds of the candidates in exactly the same way as images of candidates begin to be built from their applications. Consequently the interview and other parts of the selection process need to be designed to collect and supply the additional information required to make good-quality decisions.

You also need to take account of the fact that each individual applicant will have their own questions about how their expectations will be met by the job and organisation. It is not possible to anticipate exactly what every candidate will want to know: an effective way of dealing with these initial questions is to provide the opportunity for them to discuss informally the aspects of the job and organisation they want to know more about. Some organisations, for example, put contact names in advertisements or additional information packs.

Information about the job

If the post has been advertised, the bare bones of the job will have been included in the text. In addition some employers send out further particulars, ranging from one sheet of paper to large quantities of material. Jobs that are being filled by recruitment or employment agencies, as a result of speculative letters or other less public means, sometimes supply limited details. At the very least, before they attend for an interview, candidates should know the purpose of the job and an outline of the main duties before being interviewed. They should be told the conditions and terms of employment, the expectation of the employer and, ideally, the skills, knowledge and experiences being sought.

Information about the process

Candidates may have more than a passing interest in what is going to happen during the interview. Research has demonstrated that providing a clear description beforehand increases the candidates' acceptance of what they are asked to do. The information also helps them prepare both mentally and practically, which helps the interview to run smoothly, allowing everyone to concentrate on the content rather than dealing with questions about the process. Contrast Examples 19 and 20.

Example 19

Letter A

Dear

Post of Secretary

You are invited to attend for an interview in connection with the above post on Tuesday, 15 March at 2.30 pm. Please report to the Main Reception Desk and bring with you certificates of any qualifications you possess.

Please confirm your ability to attend.

Yours sincerely

P W Green

Personnel Officer

Example 20

Letter B

Dear

Post of Secretary

You are invited to attend for an interview in connection with the above post on Tuesday, 15 March at 2.30 pm. Please report to the Main Reception Desk at 2.20 where you will be met by Ms Tranter. Your interview will begin at 2.30 and will last approximately 40 minutes.

You will be interviewed by myself, Mr Willoughby, the Accounts Manager, and Mrs Peters, the Senior Executive Secretary. The interview will be in three parts. The first part will concentrate on exploring your general work experience. During the second you will be asked questions about your secretarial skills. The third part of the interview will give you the chance to question us and for us to ask you questions about how you see yourself in the job.

As we will need to check your qualifications, please bring with you any certificates you have.

We are looking forward to meeting you soon. If you are unable to attend on the day or time given above, please let me know as soon as possible so that alternative arrangements can be made.

Yours sincerely

Patricia W Green

Personnel Officer

The quantity and quality of the information sent to candidates in advance will also influence the way in which they present themselves for interview. Letter A will probably result in the candidate arriving promptly at the Reception Desk for 2.30 pm. but late for the actual interview. The second letter may seem lengthy but the candidates will know when to be where and will have been able to prepare themselves. Knowing they will have the opportunity to question the interviewers, they will also have had the chance to think about what they want answering. Telling candidates who will be interviewing them also helps them to prepare themselves.

Information about the organisation

Candidates need some basic information about the job for which they are applying and the organisation they are hoping to join. Some employers send information to applicants outlining the terms and conditions of the employment contract and in some cases the 'fringe' benefits provided, such as staff facilities or car parking. In addition to general information, some send shortlisted candidates supplementary information. This may include more sensitive information or details such as the company's Annual Report, business plans, product profiles and so on. How many employers tell potential employees what it is like to work for them?

Providing information about the organisation's values, its culture and normal patterns of behaviour is rare. However, it does give candidates some insight into the normal way of life that makes the organisation different from all other employers.

Ways of doing this could include:

❏ sending candidates copies of recent editions of the staff newsletter
❏ asking an existing member of staff to 'write' to the potential new employees telling them what it is like to work for the organisation
❏ encouraging candidates to arrange pre-interview visits
❏ having conversations with key individuals.

PREPARING THE OTHERS INVOLVED

Other staff who are not members of the interview panel will be involved to a greater or lesser extent in the interviews. Make sure everyone involved, at whatever stage of the process, understands their role and its limits. They also need to know what they will be required to do, when, and where, and how much time to commit to the whole process. Individuals may also need to develop the skills they will be asked to use.

Two of the biggest barriers to improving the quality of interviews are:

1. Managers who are not prepared to dedicate the time which appointing staff warrants. Rushing into the interview room minutes ahead of the first candidate is not good practice.
2. Managers who do not recognise that interviewing is a skilled process and those skills are acquired and developed only as a result of training, practice and review. The skills do not come automatically with the manager's desk and pay cheque. Similarly the process and others involved need to be prepared.

Many managers think they have more important things to do, but, unless they put in the effort, even the approaches regarded as being the 'best' will have little chance of working. Appointing the right person depends on the people involved not only doing the right things: they must do things right.

Interviewers

The interviewers are responsible for:

❑ preparing to interview
❑ conducting the interview
❑ using the role outline, job description and person specification to assess potential
❑ asking and answering questions
❑ observing candidates' behaviour
❑ rating observations against criteria
❑ note taking and record keeping
❑ reporting observations
❑ making decisions
❑ feeding back to candidates.

To ensure that these tasks are carried out properly, each interviewer needs to possess certain information about the job:

❏ its purpose
❏ where the job fits into the overall organisation
❏ the level of the job (novice or expert)
❏ the knowledge, experience, skills and attributes essential for immediate effective performance, and those which are desirable
❏ standard of performance expected
❏ the main duties and tasks
❏ training, development and career opportunities
❏ benefits – results and achievement as well as pay, perks and other rewards.

They also need to understand their exact role in the overall process. It is their job to:

❏ ask questions and obtain certain information from the candidates
❏ assess the level of the candidates' knowledge and abilities and the relevance of their experience
❏ decide whether the candidates would fit into the existing team and organisation
❏ judge the suitability of the candidates' for employment.

They should understand where the interview fits into the overall selection process. It could be:

❏ a preliminary exchange of information
❏ a screen of candidates to decide who should go through to later stages
❏ the final meeting before the decision to appoint or not to appoint is made.

Interviewers should also appreciate the limits of their authority:

❏ Are they empowered to make statements about conditions of employment and contractual matters?
❏ Are they there to make recommendations to the decision makers?
❏ Are they to make the decision regarding who or who not to appoint?

They should understand and have been trained appropriately in the techniques they are to use. If at all possible, they should be directly exposed to the technique so they know what it feels like for themselves.

Example 21

A group of garages in a middle-size market town decided to form a consortium to recruit and train their sales staff. They had found that this group of employees were highly mobile around the town, resulting in high recruitment costs, low commitment to the employer and high retraining costs. The reason the staff moved was more to do with tradition and boredom than any real dissatisfaction, as the conditions and pay rates were largely comparable.

The employers decided the solution was to start a training scheme which would include job rotation, providing shared experience, opportunities for team working and an element of competition as a way of raising standards. The scheme was supported by the TEC and launched in a blaze of publicity. As predicted, the response was enormous – over 200 letters were received.

The group had employed a recruitment consultant to help handle the response and design the selection process. The group were concerned that having received such good publicity, the interview should not leave anyone feeling as though they had 'failed', so they decided that, at each stage, candidates would be offered debriefing and feedback.

To achieve the objectives, the consultant recommended the following process:

❏ The applications would be screened against the person specifica-tion by the consultant's staff.
❏ Those not progressed would be sent a letter telling them where they and the specification had not matched, in a factual way.
❏ The long-list of 50 would be invited to one of the garage show-rooms in groups of 10 to meet existing staff and hear a pre-sentation outlining the training scheme and explaining the conditions of employment.
❏ The applicants would be asked to take some basic skills tests to check levels of numeracy and literacy.

Continued on next page

Continued from previous page

❑ They would have the chance to meet existing staff to ask questions about the job and the garages involved in the scheme.

❑ Staff would be provided with information about the scheme and rehearse the answers to likely questions.

❑ Staff would also be given some basic training as those candidates who did not progress would be offered the opportunity to receive feedback.

❑ The candidates would take part in a situational interview which would be designed to explore their interpersonal and customer-handling skills.

❑ The recruitment consultants would design the interview using the person specification to provide the criteria, and the experiences of existing sales staff to develop the situation.

❑ Sales-room managers would be asked to go through the interview to validate the questions, provide model answers and to find out what it would feel like.

❑ The managers practised interviewing volunteer sales staff. They would be trained to score against the criteria and rating scale and to report their findings.

❑ The sales staff would be offered feedback to help their development.

The consultant was happy all the key players would be ready to face the applicants, knowing that they would be participating in a designed process.

From the 50 long-listed candidates seen during the open day, 20 were asked to attend a final interview from which 8 people would be employed. The members of the four interview panels were also trained to follow the structure designed to ensure consistency. Each panel had three members: a sales room manager, an existing member of staff who would act as mentor for the trainees and a garage manager who would be the main decision maker.

The cost of the recruitment, selection and training scheme had been calculated by the consultant and compared to the previous year's estimated turnover and training expenditure. The effect of complaints and the quantity of lost business caused by poor-quality customer service were also calculated. The garage owners and managers decided that on balance the amount of money they would contribute to the trainee scheme would be recouped over 18 months. On this basis they decided to go ahead and monitor the achievement of the scheme.

The other people involved

Example 21 shows how important it is that the other people involved directly in the interview process should understand their role and its limits, and be trained to carry out their tasks. These other people can include the person who will meet the candidates at the reception desk, staff involved in informal meetings, and almost anyone else who will come into contact with the candidates outside the formal interviews.

Everyone around the area where the interviews are taking place should be aware which rooms are being used when, and what facilities are being reserved for the candidates. They should also be aware that candidates might get lost, confused and be under some stress. This may cause some of them to ask what seem to be stupidly obvious questions or to ask the same question to different people, seeking reassurance. They may get lost in a well-signed building, misunderstand simple directions, misread times and written instructions or simply not follow what is being said to them. Rather than indicating incompetence, this sort of behaviour is more likely to be a product of the abnormal situation of being interviewed.

Candidates should not be protected or isolated from other employees. The successful candidate will meet them eventually. It is important that the interviewees get a feel for the organisation and see evidence of its culture. This may include watching how people normally dress at work, how they treat each other, examples of artefacts (such as notice-boards, working spaces, equipment) and the facilities available for staff (such as staff rooms, crèche, support services).

Support staff

It is likely that other staff will be more closely involved in the interviews. They will be responsible for the administration and 'ferrying' candidates between rooms, especially if sequential interviewing is used. These staff need to be briefed and prepared to carry out their duties. They should know who is to be where, when and understand what the candidates are being asked to do.

They will need an outline of the total process so they can explain, if asked by the candidates, how one particular set of interviews fits into the whole.

The support staff should also be prepared to answer other questions from candidates. It is possible that they will be asked about the job and the organisation and the people employed. They should know what questions they should not answer and how to avoid being pressurised into giving replies they are not able to provide. Inappropriate questions asked of support staff may include details of the contract, information about other candidates or confidential information about the organisation's business and its existing staff.

SPECIAL CONSIDERATIONS

There are different views about the meaning of equality. Some believe it means that everyone should be treated in exactly the same way. Others argue that some people should be given special consideration. The reason for this is because they have, in the past, been treated less favourably than others. This less favourable treatment has largely concerned making judgements about individuals' abilities on grounds that have nothing to do with the person in question. Many are made on the basis of assumptions and stereotypes. These may be false but have been built up over a number of years to such an extent that they may generally be believed to be true. For example many still believe that it is a man's duty to be the bread winner for the family and the wife, if she works at all, should only work part time for pin money.

In some situations, acting on assumptions and stereotypes can lead to a breach of the law. It is illegal to discriminate against an individual on grounds of colour, religion, race, nationality, marital status, gender and disability. Despite the existence of these laws for over 20 years, members of traditionally disadvantaged groups still experience unfair treatment, particularly in employment. Many measures have been taken under the auspices of equal opportunities policies to help members of these groups redress the effects of unfair treatment. Some success has been achieved in removing a lot of the overt discriminatory practices. Nevertheless indirect discrimination is widespread, if not pervasive. It is no accident that:

> *There are about twice as many full-time workers who are men as there are women, and the majority of the total increase in full-time employment over the last year was taken up by men... Only a small minority of male workers are part-time, whereas just under one-half of women work part-time.*
>
> Labour Market Quarterly Report, November 1995

The effects of discrimination are also felt by members of non-white communities. Unemployment in 1995 stood at 17.7 per cent for members of these groups, while the figure for white people was 8.3 per cent.

The typical actions taken to ensure that recruitment and selection does not contravene legislation include the use of:

❑ job descriptions and person specifications to make explicit the experience, knowledge, abilities and aptitudes needed for adequate performance of the job
❑ assessment methods which allow judgements to be made based on what candidates are actually able to do
❑ training of interviewers
❑ monitoring the effects of action.

Because of the lack of impact these measures have had on the distribution of men and women and black and white people in the workforce, the emphasis has gradually changed to one which draws attention to exploring how employers will benefit strategically from valuing diversity. The way in which interviews are conducted is central to this change of emphasis. Unless candidates who have the skills, knowledge and expertise needed for the future, but whose different background may have previously barred them from being appointed, are employed, an organisation might well disadvantage itself. Positive action aimed at valuing diversity and recognising difference does not mean that members of previously disadvantaged groups are given preferential treatment: it requires the employing organisation to be even more clear about its needs. In this way, stereotypical images, false assumptions and prejudices do not get in the way of the best candidates being appointed.

Stereotypes, prejudgements and assumptions

Stereotypes

A stereotype is a generalised characteristic which is applied to all members of a group regardless of whether that feature is true for the particular individual or not. For example, a common stereotype is that the average man is aggressive and the average woman gentle. In reality, this is not true; some men are gentle and some women are aggressive. If stereotypes are used during interviews as a basis for judgement, some very wrong and dangerous decisions can be made.

Example 22

One company decided that it really needed a whiz-kid to sort out the computer problems it was facing. An advert was placed in *Computer Weekly* but the response was disappointing. Of the 20 applicants only six met the specification. They were all invited to attend an interview, but some of the appointment panel were unhappy seeing one of the candidates. He adequately met all the elements required for the job and had an excellent work history. The problem was his age – 53 years old. The other candidates were all in their 30s, graduates with well-produced CVs. Some members of the panel felt that the first candidate would not be able to cope with the demands of a fast-moving company nor keep up with the changes that were going on in the market place, so there would be no point in interviewing him. They wanted a younger person who would have new ideas and energy.

After the interviews, the panel was even more divided. The older candidate had performed very well but so had one of the younger men.

Continued on next page

> Continued from previous page
>
> Half the panel wanted the latter and half the former and the arguments for both were convincing. Eventually, the chair of the panel gave way to the case for the younger candidate. She was swayed by the point that he would have a chance of a longer career with the company than his older counterpart.
>
> Events later proved that this was a false assumption. The appointee was sacked after a year. He had spent thousands of pounds on new software, installed it without consultation with his end-users, and caused chaos. The company's trading figures were beginning to show signs of the problems. Meanwhile the older candidate had been appointed by a competitor. It was reported that he had introduced the required changes gradually and carefully, after full consultation with his 'customers'. His new employers were doing were nicely – thank you.

Using stereotypes, rather than gathering evidence from individuals about their abilities, can lead to costly mistakes. It is not easy to suspend judgement for it is normal to predict what an unknown person will look like and how they are likely to behave. That is why it is so important that major decisions, especially those concerning appointments, make use of data-gathering techniques that are known to be good predictors of subsequent performance.

Prejudgement

The words 'prejudice' and 'prejudgement' have the same roots: both imply that decisions are made in advance. As the whole process of selection involves making decisions about the applicants on very small amounts of detail, care is needed to ensure that it is possible to discriminate between those candidates who do not meet the criteria and those who are likely to do the job. Difficulties occur when decisions are made on factors other than job-related criteria.

For example, it is generally assumed that a graduate is more intelligent that an individual who left full-time education at 18. This explains why a degree is often seen as a minimum requirement. However, there are many reasons why one individual may not have taken a degree. These may be for financial or circumstantial reasons. Using a non-specific criterion such as a general educational attainment, when it is not needed for the job, may well deprive the employer of capable and clever people.

For fun, let's compare appointing staff to the business of dating agencies.

Example 23

Dating	Appointing
Individuals wishing to be registered with a reputable agency complete forms and give personal details to a trained interviewer	Applicants complete an application form or submit brief CVs
Individuals are matched by an independent party who compares features sought by one party and the features offered by another	Candidates are shortlisted against criteria, sometimes these have been specified, other times they exist only in the shortlister's head
A meeting is arranged	Shortlisted candidates are interviewed
Further meetings occur if the first is successful for both parties	Some candidates are rejected, usually without being told why
Information is exchanged as the relationship develops over a period of time	The chosen individual is made an offer and is expected to enter a legal contract
If it is possible to agree mutually satisfactory terms, a contract is formed	

Prejudgements can be dangerous. If an aggrieved candidate can prove decisions have been made on the basis of colour, religion, race, nationality, marital status, gender or disability, the employing organisation and the manager may face prosecution, and the organisation's business reputation may be damaged beyond repair.

Example 24

Fred knew what he wanted and equally what he did not want. As his small business was doing very well he did not want to disturb the closely-knit team. When Lucy, one of the machinists left, Fred advertised in the local paper, fully expecting to appoint someone who would fit in as well as Lucy had. The advert was clear about the skills and experience needed which made it easy for Fred to go through the letters. He picked out five women for interview. There was no point in even thinking about the men who had applied; they would not be neat enough, and anyway one man in a group of women would be disastrous!

Fred had been on an interviewing course at the local college and knew he had to be fair. As soon as the candidates arrived for the interview, they were met by the supervisor who asked them to do a piece of work. The best by far was done by a woman called Vivien. Fred hit the roof when Vivien, a six-foot, 25-year-old man, walked into the room. He could barely contain himself – there was no way Vivien would get the job.

A woman called Mavis was appointed. Her work was okay but not as neat as Vivien's. She also had an embarrassing personal problem. After six weeks of tolerance, the other machinists demanded that Mavis be sacked. She smelt. Fred had no choice. He could either dismiss Mavis or risk the productivity and goodwill of his other workers. He decided on the former and had to start again. Production fell, mistakes and wastage rose and all the staff felt unsettled.

Vivien complained to an industrial tribunal and was eventually awarded considerable damages. The cost of the case, the bad publicity and lost production nearly ruined Fred. If only he had appointed by best person for the job when he had the chance.

Assumptions

Assumptions are different from prejudgements. Assumptions are used to help us predict what may to happen and what an unknown person is likely to look like and do. We form assumptions from our experience and what we have been told.

Example 25

When preparing to meet a Japanese person, it would not be unreasonable to assume from what is generally known about Japanese people that they are likely to be small, quiet and bow on meeting. A 6-foot 18-stone rugby player would be a surprise.

As well as the information we acquire before meeting a new person, we depend on certain pieces of data gathered very quickly during the first few minutes of meeting. This data is gathered both consciously and unconsciously. It is reported that we make our minds up about a new person within 30 seconds of meeting them. Chapter 5 discusses how we gather and process that data, and looks at some common mistakes we all make when forming conclusions about other people.

Disabilities

Disabled people require special consideration: often we focus on what they cannot do rather than concentrate on their abilities. It can be argued that the vast majority of normal adults have some form of disability that impedes their performance. How many people have perfect eyesight, hearing and are fully physically fit? Moreover, there are areas of activity where an individual has no skills or could improve dramatically on those aspects of performance. These inabilities do not debar most people from employment. Nor do they lead to the individual being stigmatised and regarded as odd. There are many disabled people who are excluded from occupying a normal job simply because they have some limitations which may not be directly relevant to the job, so they are unable to display their other talents.

The 1944 Disabled Persons (Employment) Act established a quota system. Employers with over 20 employees were required to employ sufficient disabled people to make up at least 3 per cent of their total workforce. Specific jobs could be identified and reserved for this group of people, hence the tradition of the one-armed lift operator, the blind telephonist and the one-legged car park attendant. This legislation was enacted at a time when disabled people were seen as 'deserving' and in need of special treatment. They had served their country during the Second World War and were due repayment in the form of access to jobs within their supposed ability range.

In the following 60 years, attitudes have shifted and the needs of disabled people changed dramatically. Most people are now disabled as a result of an illness or accident occurring at or after birth or caused by some form of developmental problem. Discrimination against this group of people has escalated. The Disabilities Discrimination Act (1995) brings the legislation nearer to the sex and racial discrimination statutes. Unfortunately experience has shown that legislation does not necessarily lead to a change in behaviour. Interviewers need examples to demonstrate the inaccuracy of stereotypes and the dangers of making judgements before actually meeting an individual. Many employers have found that some of their common assumptions are totally false. For example, it is known that when compared to staff who are not regarded as disabled, disabled people rarely take time off unnecessarily, are hardworking, diligent and loyal employees.

Example 26

Pat had only one arm and leg as a result of a birth defect. Even though her hand and foot were not fully formed, she had developed a talent in sculpting, metalwork and photography. With the use of specially adapted tools and holding devices, she had produced pieces that attracted acclaim. She had collected prizes and qualifications as she moved through the various government-aided employment schemes. Eventually the schemes ran out and she was forced to rely totally on state benefits. Pat's efforts to convince employers that the examples in her portfolio were all her own work had failed repeatedly and her testimonials fell on deaf ears.

Very few disabled people really want special treatment. However, everyone has the right to the opportunity to demonstrate what they are able to do. What sort of action can employers take to ensure that disabled people are treated fairly and assessed on their abilities? Examples of positive measures can include the following:

❑ Encourage candidates to say if they need any special arrangements for the interview.

❑ Be prepared to be surprised: people's talents can outstrip expectations. Not all disabilities are physical; some, for example diabetes and epilepsy, have no visible signs and can be well controlled with medication.

❑ Be prepared to be imaginative about how the job can be done. The Department of Education and Employment through the Access to Work scheme will supply aids and adaptations to help a disabled person gain or remain at work, providing the employer takes some action as well. This can include the supply of minicom or amplifying telephones, special desks and chairs, alteration to the height of workstations, enlarging computer monitors and many other practical actions.

❑ Be prepared to change the location if an individual has problems in gaining access to the buildings where the interview is to take place.

❑ Remember to make sure that all candidates can hear the questions. Speak clearly and look directly at the candidate so they have a chance to lip read. Make sure that interviewers' faces are visible, for example by not letting them sit with their backs to the windows.

❑ Be ready to allow extra time for reading material, such as test instructions, in case the person has sight or reading difficulties such as dyslexia. Use clear print of a size which is easy to read.

❑ Do not ask questions that you would not put to someone who is not as disabled. Travel to work arrangements, for example, are the business of the individual, not the employer.

❑ Do not patronise the person. A person on crutches can shake hands and repeated offers of unneeded help can get boring.

SUMMARY

The purpose of the interview is to enable the employer and candidates to exchange information so they can make good-quality decisions about who to appoint and whether to accept the offer of the job. An effective interview, therefore, is one in which the flow of information is efficient and sufficient for the purpose, the right information is transmitted by the sender and the contents understood by the recipient. Getting this process to operate well means the person who is responsible for it has to be ready to invest some time and energy in its preparation.

What to prepare?

❏ Make sure the candidates have sufficient information about the job for which they are applying.
❏ Information about the organisation and its culture is also helpful.
❏ The candidates also need to know what is going to happen to them during the interview so they can prepare themselves adequately. This shared understanding should mean that neither wastes the other's time.

Who needs to be prepared?

❏ The person responsible for the interview and the appointment needs to plan their role and actions.
❏ Other interviewers also need to be briefed about their role, the job and its location in the organisation, how the interview is to be conducted, its place in the selection process and the questions they and the other interviewers will be asking.
❏ Interviewers benefit from being trained in:
 — questioning techniques
 — observation and listening skills
 — rating behaviour against performance criteria
 — note taking
 — reporting
 — making appointment decisions
 — giving feedback to candidates.

❑ Other people inevitably are involved in the interview, in the capacity of support staff, or simply because candidates may approach them for directions, information or help. These staff should be aware of what is happening and the extent of their involvement in the interview. Support staff require more in-depth briefing and preparation so they can make a positive contribution.

Some candidates deserve special consideration

Their particular needs are not necessarily any fault of their own. It may be that, as a result of previous discrimination, their presence in the workforce has been under-represented. A manager can take some simple steps to correct this imbalance and comply with the anti-discrimination legislation. The first of these measures is to become more aware of the roots of discrimination. The avoidance of stereotypes, assumption and prejudgements can go a long way towards ensuring that candidates are assessed fairly against job-related criteria on their abilities to perform the job to the required standard.

Some people do merit more direct action to help them find suitable employment and contribute their talents. Disabled people may need special help to enable them to demonstrate to an employer what they are able to offer. An employer may find that this action results in an employee whose contribution outstrips that normally expected of a fully able individual and so the effort could pay dividends.

4

CONDUCTING THE INTERVIEW

Conducting an interview should be like painting by numbers if you are properly prepared. This chapter considers the various aspects of the interview that benefit from early preparation. Some of these may seem obvious, but if left until the candidates are at the door, they can have a negative effect on the process. A checklist, such as the one given at the end of this chapter, will help to make sure everything is planned and some of the less obvious considerations remembered.

Frequently overlooked is the choice of venue and its layout; this can affect the atmosphere of the interview and how candidates respond. The room can feel forbidding, formal, relaxed or cosy, depending on how the furniture is arranged and how the interviewers behave towards the candidates.

Interviewing can be stressful for candidates and interviewers alike, so take account of this in the timing of the interviews and briefing of the interviewers. Stress levels also influence how interviewers behave towards the candidates; developing skills in how to question and supply information to candidates will smooth the flow and help interviewers improve their performance. Of course, question technique, active listening and observation skills benefit managers in other areas of their work, too. The way in which the interview is ended also has an effect on the candidates and may well effect whether the desired candidate decides whether to accept the offer of employment or reject it.

Planning the venue

A conducive climate is vital for an interview to be efficient. If the atmosphere and setting are right no one will notice; if they are wrong, the whole process can be wrecked.

Example 27

A Managing Director was interviewing for a new personal assistant. He wanted to be sure that the candidates understood that the role was critical to his own and would see being a PA as being a partner, not a subordinate. He decided to use the final interview to communicate this message in both its setting and conduct.

Consequently he re-arranged the furniture in his office to create a less formal setting. Two settees were moved opposite each other, with a low coffee table between. He decided to sit opposite the candidates, the Head of Office Services would sit next to them and the Personnel Officer would sit next to him. But he forgot to take account of the effects of the design of the settees. Each candidate, in turn, was mortified as they sank into deep, soft cushioned sofas and found themselves peering over their knees at their prospective employer. Some were further embarrassed as they tried, unsuccessfully, to stand up gracefully in their stylishly tight skirts and high-heeled shoes.

The Managing Director wondered why seemingly good candidates had stumbled through a relaxed interview. He was equally bemused when he received a letter from the Equal Opportunities Commission, telling him that complaints of misconduct and harassment had been received.

The interview room

Example 27 demonstrates how even the best intentions can go wrong. Careful planning requires the location to be viewed through the eyes of the interviewees as well as the interviewers. The following questions may help you do this:

❑ Where is the interview to be held – in an office, a meeting room, elsewhere on the employer's premises, in a neutral venue such as a hotel?

❑ How is the interviewee to get to the room – what direction, signing, guiding is needed from the initial point of entry?
❑ How will they get into the room – are they expected to knock and wait, will someone show them in, where will they wait if they are early?
❑ How will the interview room be set out – how will the setting effect the flow of the discussion, will the candidates be able to see the interviewers' faces?

Possible layouts

Formal setting
(interrogation)

| I | I | I |

| |

| C |

Informal setting
(discussion)

| I |

| C | ◯ | I |

| I |

Informal setting
(no table, nowhere to write, exposed knees

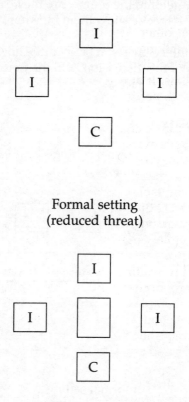

Formal setting
(reduced threat)

In the first layout, it is likely that the discussion will be a formal question and answer session. It will be harder for the interviewers to get the interviewee to engage in a flowing discussion. In the second, especially if the table is low, the discussion will be easier but interviewers may find it more difficult to ask probing questions. They may also find it more difficult to get a talkative interviewee to stay to the point. The third may inhibit the flow of the interviewee as they may feel vulnerable.

Generally, especially in formal situations, people seem to prefer a solid surface to lean on and, perhaps, to hide behind.

Expecting interviewees to sit with knees exposed 'full frontal' to the interviewers may cause them some unnecessary discomfort. The fourth layout may be the best option. The interviewers and interviewees are seated, as equal partners, round a table in full eye view of each other. The desk or table provides space for leaning and note taking and provides cover for shaking knees, tapping toes and the discreet wringing of handkerchiefs in nervous, sweaty palms. It also gives some protection for the interviewers ... yes both parties can feel vulnerable and under some stress.

The type of furniture and size of the room will also have some impact. As the above example demonstrated, soft chairs around a low coffee table may be intended to be comfortable, but hard desk chairs around the same table will seem odd. Sitting on a low chair behind a high table with the interviewers on normal sized chairs can make a candidate feel inferior. Chairs spread far apart round an enormous board table will make the interview room feel cold and remote. Four chairs huddled in one corner of the same room, with loads of empty chairs, could make everyone feel as though they are waiting for the last bus home. Four people cramped into a broom cupboard type office full of computers and files will hardly complement a free-flowing discussion. A few moments thought about the appropriateness of the room and the position of the chairs and tables can change the interview from a stultified embarrassed affair to an open free-flowing exchange of information.

The seating of the candidates in relation to the interviewers should also be seen in the context of the other fittings, spaces and effects of the room.

❏ Is the candidate going to be expected to walk over a vast empty expanse of floor to get from the door to their seat?
❏ Will the person leading the interview stand to greet the candidate and guide them to their seat?
❏ Will the floor covering produce hollow echoes of footfalls?
❏ Do the chair feet squeak on the floor?
❏ If the candidate is offered a drink, is there any where for them to put it down?

❑ Will the candidate be sat with a bright light or window facing them so that the interviewers (interrogators by now) are outlines of heads in shadow?

Waiting Rooms

The areas where interviewees are to wait also merits a few moments thought. It is normal for interviewees to be early for their appointment; providing somewhere comfortable for them, with perhaps reading material, drinks and easy access to cloak-rooms, can reduce their stress and demonstrates the employer's consideration. If candidates are taking part in a series of inter-views, they will need somewhere suitable to wait in between.

Rooms for other activities

If the candidates are being asked to do other tasks, suitable rooms, furniture and equipment need to be available. If, for example, candidates are to complete a case study, make a pre-sentation of their findings and recommendations to the interview panel and answer questions, they need somewhere quiet to work, a desk and chair, pencils, paper, possibly a calculator or com-puter, presentational aids such as overhead transparency slides, flip chart paper and suitable pens. They also need adequate time to carry out the task.

Similarly, if candidates are to perform a work sample, they will need access to all the equipment and facilities normally available. They also need to be protected against distractions and inter-ruptions. Considering that they are under abnormal pressure and probably conscious of being watched, extra time and opportu-nities for questions should be allowed. It may be helpful to candidates and the process, for a member of staff to be available to respond appropriately to questions and provide guidance.

Heating, ventilation, lighting and other considerations

A hot, stuffy, over-bright room can create an uncomfortable environment for the candidates. The interviewers, closeted for some time, could find that the heat and airlessness will have a detrimental effect on their concentration levels, patience and tolerance. By the end of a hot afternoon of interviewing the atmospherics may be less than tolerable. Likewise, a cold, dim, gloomy room will not produce the relaxed atmosphere that encourages discussion.

External factors beyond the interviewer's control can also have an impact. For example, bad weather may turn a normally pleasant room into an icebox. Thinking about how the interview room's climate may affect candidate performance may result in a change of room. Even though this may cause some inconvenience to the interviewers, the overall benefit to the process should be the prime consideration.

Interruptions

An interview should never be interrupted; it implies that other things are more important than the appointment. Telephones should be redirected, bleepers and mobile phones left outside the room and the door should be 'guarded'. Secretaries and others should be instructed to keep away likely sources of distraction. Interruption destroys the interviewers' concentration, so damaging their memories and recollections of the candidates. Even though this may seem obvious, horror stories such as interviewers signing letters while others ask the candidates questions, phone calls made in between candidates and quickie meetings are not unknown.

Timetabling

Planning the timing of the interviews and other activities is a key part of preparation. Many well-designed interviews fail to achieve their purpose either because they have had insufficient time allowed or the time available has been poorly managed. On average, an interview should last between 30 and 60 minutes. An interview lasting over one hour is long. A common approach to interview planning is for the manager to say: 'Give each candidate 40 minutes; I can spare an afternoon. If we start at 1.00 p.m. we can see 6 candidates and be done by 5.30.' The reality is likely to be:

Start	12.45	
Candidate 1	13.05	(It took longer than planned to decide who was asking which question)
Candidate 2	13.45	
Candidate 3	14.35	(Candidate 2 had a lot of questions)
Candidate 4	15.20	(One of the interviewers had to go to the toilet)
Candidate 5	16.10	(Candidate 4 had a lot to say that interested the panel)
Candidate 6	17.00	(The panel needed a drink)

At 17.45 the last candidate was somewhat unamused and members of the panel were so tired they could not remember what the first candidate looked like, and one was worried about being late for an evening appointment. They tried to reach a conclusion amid bickering and disagreement, and by 18.30 they decided on a compromise, but no one was really happy with the decision or the process.

A more reasonable time table would have been:

11.00	Candidate 1
11.50	Candidate 2
12.40	Candidate 3
13.30	Break
14.30	Candidate 4
15.20	Candidate 5
16.10	Candidate 6
17.00	Decision making

The ten-minute gap allows for slippage, assessment of the candidate, record making, comfort breaks and refreshments. The one-hour lunch break permits 'brain space' and time for consolidation.

The amount of time devoted to the first example was $5\frac{3}{4}$ hours unbroken; the second example required 6 work hours with a one hour break. The negative features of the first would possibly taint the resultant appointment and could have led to the loss of Candidate 6. The extra $1\frac{1}{4}$ hours in the second example would produce a more managed, professional interview schedule. At the end interviewers may have been tired (interviewing does demand effort) but they would not have been as exhausted as they would from the first.

PUTTING CANDIDATES AND INTERVIEWERS AT THEIR EASE

The interviewers

Getting the interviewers together, about 15 minutes before the first candidate is due is worth the time commitment. It makes sure that everyone is there on time and provides the opportunity for any last-minute questions to be sorted out. It also helps to settle the interviewers into their roles. Even for experienced interviewers this is important as meeting new people in informal settings contains some stresses, and in the formal situation of an interview these tensions can be increased. The importance of any interview cannot be over-estimated and most interviewers are aware of the far-reaching consequences of their decisions on themselves, their staff, colleagues and customers. Good interviewers are also aware of the consequences of their decisions on the lives of candidates. It is not surprising therefore that most interviewers will be a little bit tense beforehand.

The room

Despite the planning, a final check of the interview room should be made during the preparatory time. Coffee cups should be cleared away, paper and pencils provided for the interviewers and a last check made of seating and lighting. Water and glasses should be available and in reach of the candidates and interviewers. Any external noises which may cause intolerable interruptions should be dealt with and arrangements made for extra heating or ventilation if they are needed.

The candidates

It is normal for even experienced interview attendees to be nervous. This should be taken into account and considerate arrangements be made for the candidates to be greeted and put at their ease. A suitable place for them to wait – hopefully for not too long – should be available.

The person with main responsibility for the interview has some critical tasks to carry out before it starts formally:

1. Welcome the candidate, introduce yourself and outline your role.
2. Break the ice by asking the candidate some general questions, for example, about their journey.
3. Ask if anything has happened to the candidate that might effect their performance during the interview. (It is not unknown for people to attend job interviews in the middle of a life crisis. Real examples include a parent with a child in intensive care and a son whose mother had died the day before.)
4. Explain to the candidate how the interview will be carried out.
5. Introduce members of the panel and explain what their roles will be in the interview.

OPENING AND WELCOME

Once the candidate has entered the interview room, been seated, made comfortable and introductions have been made, the interview starts for real. You need to create an appropriate climate from the beginning so that the candidate will be willing to 'open up' and feel able to ask the questions they need answering. The opening few minutes are when the candidate and the interviewers build rapport and form their first impressions of each other. The interviewers need to be wary and try to keep their minds open: the dangers of stereotyping, prejudging on limited amounts of information and making assumptions were discussed in Chapter 3. More pitfalls will be explored in Chapter 5.

ACQUIRING INFORMATION

After the opening, the first part of the interview is to acquire information from the candidate. Chapter 2 looked at different forms of interview that can be used for this purpose. Regardless of the form, some tips apply equally:

1. Each candidate should be treated in the same way.
2. They should be asked only questions that relate to the job.
3. There is no need to be too formal; it is not an interrogation.
4. Ask only one question a time.
5. Don't talk too much. A common pitfall for interviewers is the temptation to fill the gaps. Short silences are okay.
6. Allow the candidate time to think and answer.
7. Be aware that the candidate will have anticipated and prepared for predictable questions.
8. Some candidates may tell lies; some will 'over-egg the cake'; others will attempt to avoid answering an unwanted question.
9. All candidates will be trying to present themselves in the best light. They are, after all, trying to promote themselves as the best candidate.
10. Do not take answers on face value. Be ready to probe, test, check and ask the same question in a slightly different way if you have any doubt about the veracity of the response already given.

Question techniques

Asking good-quality questions requires skills and preparation. However, reading out questions scripted in advance leads to stilted, rigid interviews. A more natural approach would be to use normal language and frame the questions around an agreed structure. It is also important to choose the right type of question as different types of question are known to elicit certain responses.

Type	Use	Example
Open	To encourage the candidate to talk broadly about a topic.	Q. Describe the most testing experience in your working life. A. It was when I was faced by a group of staff who were extremely angry about the way they were being treated by the organisation.
Probe	To encourage the candidate to talk in greater depth about a topic.	Q. How did that make you feel? A. I was really threatened and was not sure how best to calm them down. I wished I could hide.
Reflective	To check that the interviewer understands correctly what the candidate has said.	Q. Am I right in thinking that you felt out of your depth? A. Yes. It was the first week of my first management job and I was not sure what had happened before to make the staff so mad.
Closed	To elicit a fact or a specific piece of information.	Q. How did you respond? A. I promised the staff that I would get someone from Personnel to come to answer their grievances.

Continued on next page

Continued from previous page

Type	Use	Example
Leading	To obtain a desired answer.	Q. Did that satisfy the staff? A. Yes. They were still not happy but seemed prepared to wait and see if I could deliver someone from upstairs.
Hypothetical	To test out possible reactions to a certain situation.	Q. How would you have responded if they were not prepared to trust you? A. I dread to think. My back was against the wall. I would have had to think of some way to convince them that I was taking their complaints seriously.
Multiple	Never – they are impossible to answer.	Q. What sort of thing do you mean? Do you think it would have had the desired result? What would you have done if they were not prepared to believe you? A. ????

Active listening

Once the question has been asked, the questioner should listen to the answer. Obvious, maybe, but this does not always happen. How many people fail to really hear the reply? Often they are busy thinking about the next question or how they would have responded to the question they have just asked. Active listening is hard work. This requires:

Concentration:

❑ listening to what the candidate is saying
❑ watching what they are doing
❑ thinking about what is being said
❑ not thinking about how you are reacting
❑ not preparing what you are going to say next
❑ keeping other things out of your mind.

Controlling your body language:

❑ using appropriate movements to encourage the speaker to say more, such as nodding, smiling, using lubricators (umm)
❑ not fiddling with paper clips, pencils or fingers
❑ not producing pages of notes
❑ not doodling.

Keeping your attention focused on the candidate:

❑ not allowing distractions to get in the way
❑ not letting your gaze stray; maintaining eye contact without staring at the candidate.

Use body language or appropriate interruptions to stop a verbose candidate from talking too much. (Remember that time needs to be managed.) For example phrases such as 'Thank you, that was interesting. We now want to explore...' or to use some form of movement (such as picking up some papers) to distract the speaker.

Observation

Another aspect of active listening is observation. What you hear and observe builds the evidence you need to make decisions. The interviewers are looking for patterns of behaviour and statements that together build a picture of the candidate's potential to do the job to the standard required.

It is possible to structure observations in a similar way to planning which questions to ask. Using the person specification as a basis for behavioural criteria, the interviewers decide who will take note of which aspect of sought-for behaviour. For example, one could look for evidence of communication skills and other evidence of planning and organisational abilities. This approach makes sure that all aspects are covered rather than relying on all interviewers trying to observe everything at once. Even so, the interviewers will have made some general and overall observations. At the end of the interview a mechanism is used to aggregate observations and build the total picture. This is normally as described in Chapter 5.

Observers need to take care that they do not fabricate evidence. Human behaviour is complex and people do not behave exactly as is expected. Sometimes they do not provide the evidence required by the interviewer, but because there is some pressure to fill in all the boxes, interviewers may find themselves thinking they have seen something that did not happen. One way of avoiding this pitfall is to look for two examples of a particular aspect of behaviour. The second should either complement or disprove the first.

Example 28

Fifteen minutes into the interview, it looked as if Peter was the best candidate yet. He was the second to last and, until he came in, the panel were getting a little concerned. All the other candidates had been disappointing. Peter seemed to offer the skills and track record the company desperately needed. The sales force was falling apart. Three sales people had left and the remaining four were very unhappy. There was no doubt why. The previous manager had not been able to cope with the increasingly aggressive market and the fierce competition from other suppliers and had left. The company wanted someone who knew the business and could bring back a unifying sense of direction to the team.

Peter had produced an impressive CV. He had worked for a leading organisation and appeared to be ready for a promotion into a more managerial role. However, one of the interviewers was puzzled. Peter had not said clearly why he wanted to move, especially since his current earnings with commission was more than that on offer.

Continued on next page

Continued from previous page

The questions had touched on this several times but Peter had skilfully side stepped. The concerned interviewer noticed that everytime this had happened, Peter's fingers had started to fiddle and he fidgeted his feet. He also avoided eye contact with the panel members. The interviewer decided that the issue should not be left. Towards the end of the interview, as she saw her colleagues warming to Peter, she decided to probe:

Q.   Tell me, Peter, exactly why do you want this job?

A.   It offers me prospects to develop my management skills.

Q.   But you will earn less money.

A.   I see that as an investment in my future.

(This was not getting to where the interviewer wanted to be, so she changed tack.)

Q.   Why do you want to leave your present job?

(Shuffling of feet and slight blush to the cheeks)

A.   Well, the prospects do not seem as good as they are here.

Q.   In what way?

A.   Er, things are not moving as fast as they seem to be here; there are more opportunities for relating to customers; more freedom.

Q.   Give me an example of what you mean?

(Clearing of throat)

A.   The Company I work for has introduced new audit systems that mean we are having to do more administrative work which means that we cannot get out into the field as much.

Q.   Do you enjoy getting out more than remaining in the office?

A.   Yes, being with customers is important to me.

Q.   But the management job will be office based. How will you cope with that?

Continued on next page

Continued from previous page

A. Oh, that will be different.

Q. In what way?

A. Err, well I will still be able to maintain regular contact.

Q. How?

The interviewer was far from satisfied by this exchange and the other panel members were less confident about Peter. Even though Peter was still the strongest candidate at the end of the interviews, the panel decided to check references before making an offer. It was true that Peter's current employers were introducing better audit checks. The sales team were suspected of fraudulently claiming expenses and were regarded as a bunch of mavericks. Peter was thought to be one of the worst. He was very much the sort of self-starter and the sort of persuasive communicator needed for aggressive selling, but not a team player. In fact the opposite; he had antagonised the administrative staff and was seen by the others as a loner.

The panel concluded that Peter was not the person for their company and decided that it would be better to repeat the recruitment exercise than to make an expensive mistake.

Evidence of behaviour can only be taken as such. It is dangerous to interpret meaning or guess motives on the basis of a candidate's action and answers in an interview. It is important to take note of what the person is seen to be doing, but not to try and guess why. It is also advisable to obtain other, collaborating evidence to confirm or contradict the picture a particular behaviour has formed in your mind. It is really important to be prepared to be proven wrong and not to discount evidence that goes against your first assessment. We will discuss further in Chapter 5 how it is normal to seek confirmation of first impressions and to be disinclined to be proved wrong. We will also look at how this leads to mistakes and errors of judgement.

Assessing portfolios

Increasingly, individuals are being encouraged to compile portfolios of evidence demonstrating their abilities. Taking portfolios to interviews has been a normal practice in some professions. A graphic designer, for example, would not dream of going to an interview without their portfolio of work. Members of other groups, such as engineers, are required to put together a log to demonstrate to their peers and seniors their readiness to be entered on the register of professional practitioners. National Vocational Qualifications require candidates for an award to be able to prove to an independent assessor that they are able to perform to the required standard across a range of units of competence.

Individuals are recognising the value of their portfolio as 'proof' of their competence for other areas of assessment. Consequently, it is likely that interviewers in other professions and occupational areas will find candidates appearing at interviews with their portfolio tucked under their arm. The document may appear in many forms – photographs, reports, diary notes, records of achievement, testimonials, appraisal reports, audio or video tapes, examples of work and may, in size, be a slim volume or a full box. If the interviewers are not expecting to be presented with such a document, they may be somewhat surprised and, being expected to assess the portfolio there and then, thrown into some confusion. The advice is:

❑ Resist the pressure to assess evidence of performance demonstrated in an unexpected mode during the interview.
❑ Recognise the unfairness. If one candidate has presented extra evidence, this will give them an advantage over the others. The interviewers can decide whether to ask the other candidates to produce such evidence, thus delaying the appointment and building in another unexpected hurdle for them, or decide not to assess the portfolio.
❑ If the decision is made to examine the portfolio, do so at a later time. Other candidates should not be inconvenienced to accommodate one individual.

❑ Be aware that the portfolio may not be all the work of the individual being interviewed.

❑ Decide in advance whether to ask the candidates to bring with them examples of their work. In this way all candidates will have the same opportunity, if not the same resources at their disposal to help them prepare their portfolio. If this course of action is followed, it is possibly fairer to provide candidates with guidance about what is and what is not expected.

Checking detail and perception

Interviewers should try to double-check the basis on which assessments are formed. The research technique of 'triangulation' is a useful aid; it simply means gathering information or evidence from two or more different sources.

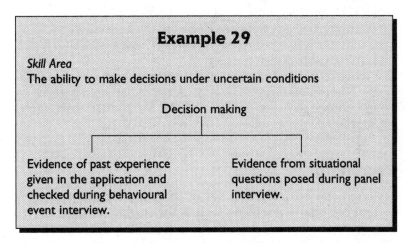

Example 29

Skill Area
The ability to make decisions under uncertain conditions

Decision making

Evidence of past experience given in the application and checked during behavioural event interview.

Evidence from situational questions posed during panel interview.

It is always worth making sure that any performance claims are accurate. As shown in Example 28, candidates can try to conceal aspects of their performance and experience that do not quite match that required. This need not be dishonesty – candidates are advised to sell themselves and try to show themselves in the best light. After all, obtaining a job is competitive and chancy.

From the interviewer's perspective it is quite normal to see people in a good light. Generally we want to see people succeed so we give them the benefit of the doubt. Generosity of this nature is to be commended except when it blinds interviewers to what could be significant areas of weakness. All too often performance problems which emerge after a couple of years of employment can be traced to suspicions noted during the interview but ignored or overlooked.

Therefore, interviewers are encouraged to:

❑ draw on at least two sources of information for evidence and assessment
❑ doubt their own judgement by asking themselves why they think what they do about each candidate
❑ check their perceptions with the other people involved in the interview
❑ look at the decision from the opposite perspective – for example, instead of saying 'these are the reasons why I think Candidate X is an able decision maker', ask why Candidate X is not an able decision maker
❑ express clearly any doubts or hesitations about a candidate to the other interviewers and consider possible consequences on the subsequent performance if the individual were to be appointed.

Recording

Making notes during the course of an interview is important. If several candidates are being seen in the session, notes help distinguish between candidates and remind the interviewers of who did and said what. Notes also form important records as they demonstrate the equity of the process, in case it is challenged at some later time.

Note taking requires skill to ensure it is unobtrusive and does not distract either the candidate or the interviewer. The record should not attempt to be a verbatim report of all that is said; rather it should briefly note the main points given in answer to the fundamental questions, evidence against the criteria and the interviewer's observations. It is worth remembering that some candidates can read upside down.

Example 30		
Candidate's Assessment Record		
Criteria	**Answers**	**Observations**
BALANCE Ability to keep overall aims in view and exercise judgement while under pressure to deal with urgent matters of detail.	Said he would deal with the urgent matters first to get them out of the way. Did not get round to the important issues.	Seemed to get thrown off course by unexpected questions. Missed the point of the question.

SUPPLYING INFORMATION

This part of the interview, unfortunately, is often neglected or compressed into a short space at the end. The candidates should be given ample time within which to ask their questions. Peter Herriot (1989) stresses, on the basis of his research, the role of the interview as a negotiation rather than a one-way verbal examination. The use of the interview to clarify understandings and harmonise expectations is known to influence the quality and success of the appointment from both parties' points of view.

Usually, this means that candidates ask polite and predictable questions about holidays, salary, training opportunities and the like. It might help if interviewers encourage candidates to explore topics by asking questions such as 'Would you like to explore with us what a typical working day here is like?' or 'Would you like us to describe the company's major markets and what our customers' expect from us?'. It is possible that candidates have been able to glean their needed information during informal visits and interviews organised before the main interview. Nevertheless checking to make sure that candidates understand as much as possible about the culture and priorities of the organisation and that they share its values is an important aspect of the appointment process. Specifically candidates need to be clear:

About the job

At the very least the candidate should have been given a description of the job for which they are being interviewed. Regrettably it is not uncommon for candidates only to have seen information such as that shown in Example 31.

Example 31

Production Editor

Books & Journals

C£16,000

London-based book publisher seeks

above to oversee the production

of all titles from manuscript to CRC.

Ideally 1–2 yrs experience.

Call May 0181 428 7163

Fax CV's 0181 429 2014

MF Publications

At the very least, candidates deserve an outline of the job and some indication of the experience and skills being sought by the employer. They should also be told about the benefits they could expect to accrue if their application is successful. These should be more than just the salary; for example it could include information that 'You will be trained in modern production techniques and be given opportunities to develop your skills and establish close working relationships with your customers'.

Some organisations send out huge volumes of literature which can be very informative or, if poorly produced, only serve to confuse and overwhelm. Regardless of what is sent out in advance, it is during the interview that the real exchange of information and clarification of understanding should take place. Part of the interview should check that the candidate's understanding of the job, the limits of responsibilities, the emphasis of the priorities and the opportunities it presents are accurate.

Over-selling a job can lead the person who is eventually employed to have unrealistic expectations which can later result in conflict. For example, rash promises of development opportunities, such as interesting projects or participation in qualification courses, could be deemed to be part of a verbal contract, and failure to deliver could be interpreted as a failure to comply or termination of the contract, which could entitle the individual to claim constructive dismissal. An extreme example, perhaps, but a caution to the interviewer who could get carried with the promise of a rosy future.

About the organisation

Conveying an image of the organisation as a place to work is not so simple. Business plans can explain to candidates the organisation's strategic direction, and profiles of services and product catalogues make sure they know the nature of the business, but communicating the culture is less easy. Some organisations have value statements and 'charters' for staff, which outline the important beliefs of the organisation, from the employers' perspectives. However, cold words on paper cannot convey the full spirit of the organisation's culture. These are found in the organisation's myths, symbols, stories of success and failure, patterns of behaviour, and can form suitable topics for discussion in small-group interviews.

About opportunities and expectations

Candidates should be given realistic pictures about the prospects contained in the job, the organisation and the standards expected. After all, the candidate and the employer are on the brink of entering a contract that, even taking account of the increasing trend towards temporary employment, might last a working lifetime. Even if information has been sent out in advance, discussing what the opportunities mean in practice gives additional clarity.

Candidates should also be able to form realistic expectations rather than just enjoy pipe dreams. A junior clerk, starting work on a training scheme, should not be allowed to believe that the office-skills course will lead *automatically* to a degree in business administration or to an MBA and a job in management. Candidates should be able to tell the difference between what is really possible and what potential really exists. They also need to be sure of their part of the bargain; the employment contract is an agreement between two parties, each of whom has rights and responsibilities to the other.

MANAGING THE INTERVIEW

Even when a carefully constructed timetable has been prepared, you must still manage time carefully, to ensure that candidates are interviewed when arranged and are given an adequate opportunity to present themselves properly. There is no point in either dragging out an interview or rushing it. If questioning and answering are exhausted before the time allocated is ended, there is little point in continuing for the sake of it.

Chairing the interview

Regardless of the form of interview chosen, one person should take or be given overall responsibility for the process. This person's role is to act as an 'overseer' and a 'sweeper'.

The *overseer* role enables the candidates' behaviour in general to be observed and any underpinning themes given in answer to specific questions noted.

The *sweeper* role would allow any unasked or avoided questions to be probed and followed up before the interview moves to the next topic. However, these roles demand that the person taking the chair has to, literally, sit back and watch. It also provides a position from which to manage the other interviewers, but it requires self-control.

Managing yourself

Even though each interviewer is responsible for his or her own conduct, the person chairing the interview needs to exercise self-restraint and limit any direct contribution to the content of the interview. It is very tempting to engage in an in-depth discussion with a candidate on a favoured topic but this may mean that a verbose candidate successfully side-tracks you and the other interviewers to the detriment of other candidates.

Managing the other members of the interview panel

It is rare that any interaction goes exactly as intended, no matter how well it was planned. This may be for various reasons.

❏ The candidate may try to avoid a question, thus requiring further probing.
❏ The candidate could introduce a topic or pose a question that merits discussion.
❏ Some aspect of the individual's application may be unclear so questions relevant only to that individual are asked.
❏ An interviewer decides in the middle of an interview to raise a new topic.
❏ An interviewer or candidate may introduce a 'red herring'.

The chair of the interview is responsible for steering its flow so that the questions that need to be asked are all raised and irrelevant topics kept to a minimum. It is also the chair's role to make sure that the other interviewers behave themselves. There are tales, hopefully exceptional, of interviewers falling asleep signing letters while candidates answered questions, and talking among themselves.

Example 32

Chris decided to take issue with one candidate. He did not agree with the principle on which the candidate had based her answer so he engaged in what developed into a heated argument over a highly specialist academic point that had little relevance to the job. It took some time for the chair of the panel to persuade Chris to let go of the point. It was a waste of time, irrelevant to the interview and inappropriate behaviour. Fortunately the candidate had the self-confidence to withstand the unnecessary onslaught and recomposed herself enough to continue with the interview. The chair of the panel remonstrated later with Chris, but it was too late to prevent the very able candidate rejecting the offer of employment.

Managing the candidates

The quarrelsome one

It is not common to find candidates arguing with interviewers, but they do, on occasions, try to take over the interview. This may be a positive sign of an assertive and confident individual, or it could be indicative of a domineering show-off.

The talkative one

Some candidates answer questions at length. Verbosity may be a sign of nervousness or an attempt to demonstrate to the interviewers the scope of the individual's knowledge and experience. The person chairing the interview has a responsibility to indicate to the candidate, tactfully, when they have answered the question adequately. This should be done carefully so the candidate is not interrupted or made to feel closed down. One way is to ask a closed question that will result in a 'yes' or 'no' answer thus enabling the next question to be posed. Another is to say something like, 'Thank you. I think you have answered X's question adequately. Now Z would like to ask you about your experience when you worked for ABC Ltd'.

It is important that candidates are not allowed to over-run. This either cuts into the time allowed for assessing a candidate or keeps the next one waiting.

The silent one

Some people find it very difficult to talk to interviewers. It may be that nerves 'caught their tongue' or that they are naturally reticent. Regardless, the interviewers have a responsibility to try to draw out the talents that may be hiding. Asking open questions can just freeze the individual, so encourage the candidate with a few leading questions to get them used to speaking. These can lead on to more in-depth questions once the candidate has built their confidence. It may be, of course, that a candidate simply has nothing to say.

The hard bargainer

Sometimes candidates will try to pin down interviewers to making commitments that they cannot keep. The chair is responsible for making sure that the panel does not fall into holes that are being dug. It is possible that candidates are more practised and skilful in this sort of negotiation than the interviewers. Any promise made can be legally binding if it is made in connection with an offer of employment. These rash commitments could include attendance on a training or qualification course, the payment of relocation costs or provision of living accommodation, or to provide certain resources, facilities or benefits, such as a car, computer facilities, secretarial help or private medical insurance. Discussion of such issues over and above those specifically provided for as part of the job should be avoided if possible in the interview. They can be picked up later after an offer has been made. The candidates are able to accept an offer subject to certain conditions and come to satisfactory agreements during the later negotiation phase in exactly the same way as an employer makes an offer subject to certain checks.

The surprising one

Sometimes, a candidate turns out to be very different from that expected.

Example 33

Q.   What sort of emergency action would you take if, as Woodland Supervisor, you found a tree damaged by high winds?

A. (in all seriousness)   I always carry a first-aid box in the back of my van and make sure it contains some very large plasters.

The interviewers had to be very careful to avoid each other's eyes and the Chair had to struggle to get the questions flowing again. To no avail. The next question, a change of tack, concerned how best to supervise a gang of workers spread out in a forest. Expecting a 'walk the job' type of reply, the interviewer was somewhat surprised to hear, 'I had this sort of problem in my last job. I found that if I tied a piece of string to each worker's ankle I could tug whenever I wanted to check up on what they were doing. It saved a lot of time and I could monitor several at once'.

The candidate also wanted to talk about irrelevant matters; nevertheless the chair felt it important to treat them seriously and with respect. The interviewers had to maintain their self-control in order to retain the candidate's and their own dignity. This situation called for all the chair's skill and much tolerance from the interviewers.

CLOSING THE INTERVIEW

How an interview is closed can have an impact on a candidate's subsequent decision. At the end of the interview all candidates should feel that they:

❏ have had an adequate chance to demonstrate their suitability for the job
❏ have been treated with respect and dignity
❏ have had the opportunity to find out what they need to know about the job, the parameters of the role, the organisation and the context in which they would be working
❏ are clear about what will happen next.

If a candidate is left with a picture of a badly run interview they will not necessarily be confident that they have been given fair consideration. They will also be left with the impression of an organisation or a manager who does not know what he or she is doing. Who wants to work in a place like that?

Leaving a good final impression is also important for the organisation's reputation. In most job interviews, only one candidate is successful, which means several, or many others will have been unsuccessful. Anyone who feels a failure, in addition to normal self-recrimination, usually tries to find external reasons to blame, such as the behaviour of the interviewers or the questions asked. If the candidates are left feeling badly treated, these may be given undue importance and influence what the candidates say to other people about the organisation. As word-of-mouth publicity is one of the main factors in creating an image, what unsuccessful candidates say about how they were treated can have an impact on the organisation's reputation as an employer. To make a candidate feel well treated, you must:

❏ make sure each individual believes that they have done their best
❏ check to make sure they know they have been given a fair hearing
❏ emphasise that the person to be appointed to the job will be the one whose experience, knowledge and/or skill levels best fit those required for the post
❏ tell the individual that not being appointed does not mean the individual is a failure or is being rejected as a person
❏ not tell the unsuccessful candidates they were a close second

❏ not explain in detail why another candidate was better
❏ offer feedback designed to help the candidates with future interviews.

Candidates have the right, in certain circumstances, to complain to an industrial tribunal if they think their treatment was in breach of a law. The chances of unfounded claims being made are reduced if care is taken in the closing stages of the interview. Closing the interview well means telling the candidates:

❏ how the 'best' candidate will be selected
❏ who will make that decision
❏ how the candidates will be told of the decision (will you tell the other candidates who has been appointed?)
❏ when the candidates will be told of the decision
❏ whether the candidates will be offered feedback, what to do if they want the feedback, who will provide it, how, and when.

If candidates are invited to wait for the decision on the day, make sure there is somewhere suitable for them to wait, they know how long they are likely to wait, and what is going to happen when the decision is announced. This will be discussed more in Chapter 6.

SUMMARY

A well-run interview:

1. is conducted in a venue that is:

    ❏ chosen with care
    ❏ adequately heated, lit and ventilated
    ❏ laid out to ease the exchange of information
    ❏ complete with adequate waiting rooms and suitable accommodation for candidates to do any set tasks
    ❏ protected from interruptions
    ❏ prepared.

2. is timed so that

   ❏ candidates are able to answer questions fully and find out what they need to know
   ❏ interviewers are able to complete the assessment and report notes for each candidate before seeing the next
   ❏ interviewers are not over-stretched and too tired. At the end of the interview they require enough mental and physical energy to give proper consideration to making overall assessments and decisions.

3. has interviewers who are settled and ready to welcome the candidates

4. has an underpinning structure with

   ❏ an opening
   ❏ a stage where interviewers acquire information through the use of well-constructed questions, active listening, observation, checking and recording evidence
   ❏ a stage when candidates can obtain the information they need about the job, the organisation, and opportunities and expectations.

5. is managed so that

   ❏ timings are maintained
   ❏ interviewers are disciplined and professional
   ❏ candidates are steered towards the desired end
   ❏ extremes of behaviour are controlled.

6. is closed so that candidates

   ❏ know what will happen next
   ❏ are offered feedback
   ❏ are left with an impression of a well-run organisation that treats its current and potential employees equally and with respect.

5

DECIDING WHO TO APPOINT

Asking candidates questions is the easy part of interviewing: making the decision is harder. Most interviewers start with the hope that when they get to the end of the interviews, they will be able to send off the last candidate with promises of an early result, and have a clear outcome. The reality is often that the decision is far from clear. Possible outcomes can include:

❑ having to choose between several equally good candidates, each of whom has very different qualities
❑ dealing with a poor bunch, none of whom is really near enough the profile to appoint
❑ having to resolve differing opinions between interviewers.

There are many dangers to trip up the unwary interviewer. These can effect the quality of the outcome by influencing and distorting the interviewers' assessment of the candidates. In this chapter we will explore how perceptions are formed and the more common errors and biases that distort them. We will also consider how some of the dynamics between interviewers can take over from the task in hand, and some simple methods that aid decision making will be described to help interviewers improve their practices.

DANGEROUS INFLUENCES

Initial impressions

Appearance

Research has demonstrated that physical appearance is one of the first things we notice about another person, hence the huge sums of money spent each year on cosmetics and beauty aids. There is also some evidence to suggest that those people regarded as being 'attractive' are deemed to be 'good'; whereas those judged as being 'ugly' are seen as 'bad'. Attractive people are 'nice', and we all like to be surrounded by nice people (it may rub off on us) and people that we like.

The definition of attractiveness is highly culturally bound, and includes undertones of sexual attraction, as most product advertisers know too well. The popular image of beauty almost automatically rules out most people with a physical disability, and can be extremely ageist. How can an interviewer deal with the appeal of an attractive candidate and the lack of appeal of a candidate seen as 'ugly'.

Other research suggests that wearing perfume, aftershave, lipstick and other make-up affects the interviewers' perceptions of candidates. Interestingly, this does not seem to be based totally on gender. A man wearing too much aftershave will have the same effect on interviewers as a woman soaked in perfume. Female interviewers react in the same way as their male counterparts. A bright shade of lipstick suggests to some interviewers that the wearer might be 'flighty'.

A person's choice of clothing also influences how they are perceived. Some interviewers believe that a women in a flowery dress will not be taken seriously, and too severe a business suit could result in her being regarded as bossy and aggressive. A man in casual or uncoordinated clothes will not be very efficient and too formal a garb may suggest that he will be after his boss's job! In addition to social conventions, the way clothes are seen will be influenced by the organisation's cultural norms.

The interviewers can find out how they react to people on first meeting by checking:

❑ What is the first thing to be noticed about the new person?
❑ Does this create a favourable or unfavourable impression?
❑ How does this effect the likelihood of the new person being liked or disliked?
❑ Does the first thing really matter?

Behaviour

How the candidate behaves on entering the room is also perceived in similar ways by the interviewers, who will each have his or her own views about what does and does not matter. These values may be totally inconsequential in the context of the appointment; nevertheless, they influence judgement. For example some people believe that a candidate should wait to be asked before sitting down, and a slack handshake means a weak character. Even though Desmond Morris' *Manwatch* is fascinating reading, it should not be used as a selection aid. Rather, interviewers should examine their own values and the way in which they interpret other people's behaviour before deciding if it matters.

Language

What the candidate says and how they say it also creates an impression. For example a strong accent or the use of dialect, in some quarters, are seen as indicators of poor levels of education. Even though TV companies have increased the number of announcers with regional accents, and there is greater acceptance of difference, we still tend to see the mid-Atlantic and South East tones as evidence of well-educated and cultured individuals.

Using patterns of speech as a source of evidence for general intelligence can lead to more damaging pre-judgements. The Industrial Research Unit explored the different ways in which people who learnt English as a second language construct their sentences. They found that those who learnt English as their first language normally start with general statements and then move to specifics. In some Asian languages the opposite is true. In the interview setting, this can make the person whose first language is not English sound over-detailed and, depending on the question, as if they are bragging.

Culture

Behaviour patterns are also grounded in culture, for example the unwritten codes of conduct about shaking hands. In some countries candidates are expected to provide proof of their qualifications at the interview; in others, the word of the candidate will be good enough. These different patterns of behaviour can lead interviewers to form wrong impressions about the candidates' abilities and base their assessment on features of behaviour that are not relevant to the job.

Motivation

Dangerous assumptions can be made concerning another person's motivation. 'Motivation' is the emotion and personality that causes an individual to behave in a certain way – the driving force behind action. The behaviour that is seen and experienced does not necessarily reflect fully or accurately an individual's reason for acting in a particular way. Behaviour can be controlled and emotions masked.

Example 34

Nelson was not amused. He had been given the wrong directions in the letter inviting him to attend an interview. The buildings were badly signed and shabby, the receptionist didn't have a clue what was happening and now he was late. When he finally arrived at the interview room, he had decided he probably would not get the job and in any case he didn't want it now the interviews were running 30 minutes late. 'What a shambles' he thought, as steam metaphorically came from his ears. But, he decided, since he was there he may as well go through with it; good experience if nothing else.

Nelson's cool, detached responses drew admiration from the frazzled interviewers. 'Just our man. What a professional. Interviews don't rattle him,' they concluded. They were foxed when they rushed out, expecting to find all the candidates waiting (eagerly) for their deliberations as they had requested. Nelson was not there to be seen. When the assistant brought in his message withdrawing his application, they were dumbfounded.

Guessing why someone behaves in the way they do, will guarantee only one result – the wrong answer. The only way to get the right answer is to ask the individual concerned. The following points will help an interviewer avoid the temptation of making judgements about candidates too soon and on the basis of superficial information:

❑ Be aware of the desire to attribute motive to action.
❑ Know what physical and behavioural features attract you to another person.
❑ Focus on the criteria needed for the effective performance of the job rather than your liking for the candidate.
❑ Explore the evidence of achievement, and look for behavioural indicators which demonstrate the candidate's action. Get behind the words.
❑ Do not let interpersonal skills and the need for social fit, as important as they are, dominate the assessment of the candidate's capability.
❑ Do not let secondary criteria take precedence.
❑ Assess the potential of future performance in the context of your organisation and the job in question.
❑ Double-check perceptions, using at least two sources of evidence and other interviewers' assessments.
❑ Check evidence for anything that disproves the opinion being formed.
❑ Do not make immediate decisions. Suspend decision making until all candidates have been interviewed and the assessment of each can be viewed with some hindsight.

Effect on interviewers' memories

One of the most common distortions that influences judgement is the interviewers' memories of the candidates. This can be a particular problem if a large number of candidates (more than six) is being interviewed in a short space of time (such as one half-day). Trying to see everyone quickly is a common pitfall. Busy managers find it difficult to spare too much time on such a low-level task and may try to get it over with fast. In practice, this means that candidates are given the minimum amount of time and little time is allowed between them. Appointments to posts such as secretaries, receptionists, operators, technicians, engineers and even junior managers are made on the basis of a half-hour chat with little exploration of their abilities to do the job and less explanation of what the job entails.

Seeing so many people so quickly means that, at the end, the manager and other interviewers will find it difficult to distinguish one candidate from another. The factors that influence their recall may have little to do with the candidates' abilities or their potential to do the job. These factors are primacy, recency, saliency and, as described above, appearance.

Primacy

The first candidate to be seen is more likely to remain more clearly in the interviewer's memory that the candidates seen later. This phenomenon is known as primacy.

Recency

Similarly, the last candidate seen will be more strongly remembered for the simple reason he or she was the last or most recent person seen. The brain is able to access the last impression more readily than those formed some time earlier and stored in the deeper memory.

Both of these factors mean that to make sure that the middle candidates are recalled equally well, the interviewers have to take steps to fix them in their minds as distinct individuals and provide some hooks to fetch them out of the memory. This may include making a note of something the person said or did. Some interviewers draw sketches, and, where large numbers of people are being interviewed, take Polaroid pictures.

Saliency

This third factor is a little more difficult to control, as it may effect the memories of the interviewers without them being aware of what is happening. A salient point is something conspicuous, that sticks out. This may be the candidate's nose! The strength of the impression created may work in the favour of the candidate but may be totally unconnected with that individual's potential ability to do the job.

Example 35

Jo had not seemed a particularly strong candidate during shortlisting. She had only been included as she had had some experience that none of the other candidates had obtained and the interviewers thought that this may be useful to the company. The other candidates called for interview seemed more appointable.

For the bulk of the interview Jo's performance confirmed the weakness of her application. However, one thing occurred during the interview that made her stand out from the rest. During the post-interview discussion all the interviewers remembered Jo clearly. The other candidates faded in comparison even though the reason Jo stood out had absolutely nothing to do with the job.

Jo had had a coughing fit in the middle of her interview. One of the interviewers had handed her a drink of water but in doing so had fallen over the carpet and tipped the water over the main interviewer. Everyone burst out in embarrassed laughter and it took some minutes before the interview could continue. Everyone had relaxed and the interview changed into a friendly discussion. On the strengths of the rapport that had been built, the interview panel decided that even though Jo did not have all the qualities they were seeking, her 'special' experience and well developed interpersonal skills made them think that she would fit in well with the organisation. Any shortfall in ability could be rectified, they concluded, by intensive training.

The effect of saliency can work against the candidate in a similar fashion. It is essential, therefore, that interviewers focus on the criteria required for effective performance on the job and are able to justify *all* their decisions against that framework. Any decisions or conclusions made on factors outside that framework need to be explored and be justifiable when the decision is examined in the light of hindsight. Interviewers should test:

❑ why they have reached a particular conclusion
❑ which pieces of evidence were used as a basis for that conclusion
❑ whether the conclusion is valid, in other words, is it a logical conclusion to draw from the evidence
❑ if the evidence and conclusion are relevant for the job.

Seeking similar characteristics

Another pull, just as strong as the desire to be surrounded by people we find attractive, is the wish to work with people like us. This desire underpins our social structure. It can be seen in the formation of tribes and how groups respond to people who do not 'fit'.

New members are attracted to a group. They either seek the group or are recruited by existing members. In the early days of membership, the new person is socialised and conditioned carefully to make sure they understand the group's norms and rules (the latter are usually unwritten). If they 'behave' well and comply they are rewarded by treats and accolades. If they reject the group's basic assumptions, they are ostracised, or punished in all sorts of subtle and painful ways. They are not included in the less formal aspects of organisational life and so they fail to gain insight into the deeper parts of the group's society such as relationships between key individuals, and most importantly the politics of the group. Consequently, they make mistakes or get set up to fail. This then leads to unhappiness, exclusion or total withdrawal and ultimately the group may expel the individual from membership. The individual may leave voluntarily or remain a member but live a half-life on the fringes of society.

How many people brought into organisations to bring about change stay for very long? After their departure the reasons given can include they could not fit in, they did not take into account the feelings of the existing staff, or they did not understand our culture. Sometimes newly appointed individuals settle in very well with the status quo but don't bring about the desired changes because they have adjusted to conform to the present position.

Example 36

The Service Department had suffered for years under the weak leadership of its manager. When Henry found another job, the MD saw the opportunity for a fresh start. Gerry did well at the interview. He had been liked by the interviewers who were also pleased with the depth of his technical knowledge and the sheer range of his service experience. Moreover, he spoke their language. The interviewers were united in the view that he would be able to bring about the changes the department needed: a good choice and a good fit.

After two months the MD began to worry. Gerry had developed exceedingly good relationships with the Service team, who respected the extent of his knowledge. They were at one with their new boss. This was good, but the quality of the service provided to the customers was just as bad. If anything the number of complaints was rising, not declining. What was wrong?

On reflection the MD saw that Gerry had been selected because he had developed a strong rapport with the interviewers who had concluded that he would fit. The bulk of the interview had focused on his technical skills, and little evidence was collected about his abilities to lead a team. But these were the very qualities needed; the team was short of management, not technical skills.

Errors

When making decisions about other people, we all make mistakes, but it is uncommon, especially in the case of job interviews, for this to be admitted. It is inevitable that some mistakes are made because the process relies on imperfect and incomplete information. We cover up by using personal devices to reduce the uncertainty caused by this lack of information and fill in any gaps for ourselves.

Rules of thumb

We each develop our own personal view of the world. Experience, lessons learnt from other people, the things we are told all influence how we interpret events and see other people. From these we built a mental image called a 'schema' and use 'constructs' which are built to help us predict how people are likely to behave in given situations. These are confirmed and refined as we go through life and provide us with mental short cuts – our rules of thumb. We can rely on these as we have used them before and know they work. They do not need to be double-checked.

Additionally, we believe that some events are more representative of life than they really are and that features of a situation or characteristics of an individual are general rather than unique.

Example 37

Didn't Julius Caesar tell us:

> Let me have men about me that are fat;
> Sleek-headed men and such as sleep o'nights;
> Yond Cassius hath a lean and hungry look;
> Such men are dangerous.

We also tend to use the most easily available evidence rather than do the mental work required to recall information or question an assumption. In other words, if something happened last week we use that as being generally applicable rather than atypical.

As an interviewer, you need to be aware of your beliefs and rules of thumb to be sure they are based on truth, not truism.

Cause and effect

We see the individuals we are interviewing as in the centre of a stage. We believe they are and have been in a position to effect all the events that have occurred around them and have caused the end results.

Example 38

A certain manufacturer of kitchen fittings had a disastrous period during which its accounts were rejected by the auditors and the financial director was accused of improper conduct. Most of the staff employed in the Finance and Accounts Department were sacked. The main reason for taking this action was to satisfy the shareholders that the MD was back in control.

A young accountant was left trying to put her career back together. She felt unfairly treated by her former employer as she had worked in the purchasing section and had nothing to do with the accountancy team. Yet she was finding that her employment history was making it very hard to convince potential employers that she was honest and competent at her job.

The tendency to attribute cause and effect to an individual has been known to lead to some disastrous appointments. If we assume that an individual who worked for a highly successful company was a lone cause of that success, we could place unreasonable demands and have unreal expectations of them and, in effect, set them up for failure.

Seeking confirmation and discounting contradictory evidence

We like our rules of thumb. We also like our first impressions and think, 'I liked Nev when we first met, I wanted him to succeed. Even though we really needed someone to be fluent in French and he could only manage a few words during the interview, it does not matter. It is just a minor flaw. He was nervous. We can sort that out with a refresher course once he starts'.

We do not like being proven wrong in our judgements about other people. But it is known that we tend to form our initial and strongest impressions during the first 30 seconds of meeting, so inevitably these are formed on very little information. These may be favourable or disadvantageous. As the interview progresses we seek evidence to confirm our initial impressions. The interviewers ask questions that indicate what answers are wanted and tend to avoid dangerous ground. Opportunities are provided for the individual to fit into the picture being painted around them. The candidate, wishing to please, responds accordingly. A candidate good at the interview game can recognise the clues and is able to give the answers being sought. Together the interviewers and candidate collude to build the picture and develop either a mutual like or dislike. It has been known for interviewers subconsciously to fabricate evidence so that the 'reality' of the candidate's suitability for the post is made to fit what is wanted.

Example 39

Bertie walked through the door of the interview room extruding confidence and professionalism. He had applied for the post of PR Manager and looked the part from the top of his perfectly groomed head to the soles of his voguishly shod feet. He strolled to the table and shook hands with each of the interview team and, in well-educated tones, bade them 'Good afternoon'. The CEO was slightly fazed by the wave of gravitas and took a few seconds to open the interview. By this time, Bertie was in charge.

The interview did not last the full amount of time allotted. It did not need to. Bertie, from the outset, was head and shoulders above all the other candidates. Besides, he ran the interview, leading the questioning through the use of skilful prompts, on to topics where he was obviously well able to demonstrate his competencies. The CEO had liked what she saw from the first moment and was quite happy to let Bertie run the interview.

She was not so happy six months later. Bertie had proved just how capable he was at interviewing; the problem was, he could not deliver. He had opened up a number of highly attractive PR campaigns but not one had actually run. On reflection, the CEO saw what had happened. Not once during the interview had any of the interviewers asked Bertie to describe a project which he had initiated and implemented.

The dangerous ground we try to avoid is that which will take us into areas which would disprove our first impressions. In Example 39, if the CEO had regained her position of leader of the interview and had used job-related criteria and a technique such as behavioural event interviewing, Bertie would not have been able to escape the more probing and challenging questions. The CEO would have had to acknowledge that her first impression of a highly competent individual was based on façade not fact.

Other peoples' opinions

During interviews we make use of other people's opinions about the candidates. References are commonly used and there are many good reasons why an offer of employment should not be made to a candidate without carrying out some checks about their application and past employment record. In Britain references and recommendations are used far more than in other European countries. More common is to ask a previous employer or someone with knowledge of the candidate's performance in a work context to express an opinion about their abilities to carry out the job for which they are being interviewed. The responses are then used as part of the evidence collected from their application, any other assessment process and the interview.

The main problem lies in what the referees are being asked to do. There is no reason why facts should not be checked with previous employers, but it is expecting a lot of someone to express an opinion about an individual's ability to perform a job they may know very little about, in another organisation with which they may not be familiar.

Case law, at one time, meant that references more or less had to be written in either bland terms or expressed as degrees of excellence. The fear of defamation resulted in referees saying little that could be challenged. Consequently, interviewers had to learn to read between the lines. Today, previous employers have a duty of care to report accurately on an individual's level of performance. But this can only be done from the previous employers' own experience of the individual concerned;

predicting how that individual will perform in a new organisation doing a new job with other people is beyond their abilities.

Relationships and circumstances may exist that neither the previous employer nor candidate would wish to disclose to a third party. Work-relationship breakdowns are common, but none of us likes to admit to them. Some bosses feel let down when their staff apply for other jobs and, if that individual is particularly valuable, may not want to help them get another job. Additionally, we all know of cases where incompetent employees are given a glowing reference to help them on their way.

Yet during the interview process, letters of reference are often given a high degree of credence. Interviewers like the comfort of their opinions being confirmed by an outsider, and if we have doubts we like to find external evidence to help us make sense of them and make them more real. The motivations behind what is said in a reference are not always obvious and therefore the worth of what is written or said by one person about another needs to be treated with caution.

To avoid giving undue weight to a reference, interviewers need to be clear what they are looking for, use appropriate means of finding the evidence and ask the right people the right questions to obtain supporting or disproving information. Rely on facts that can be substantiated and double-check opinion.

Escalation

Another factor to influence the outcome of an interview is the amount of time that has already been invested. Interviewers feel that, since they have invested much time and energy, even if they begin to have doubts, they are obliged to continue to the expected outcome. If, at the end of the interview, none of the candidates matches the requirements, interviewers can feel some pressure to appoint someone rather than no one. Similarly if a long time has been spent with one or two of the candidates, it is hard to pull back.

Example 40

Before the formal interviews, and on paper, two scientists seemed to be highly appointable but during the interviews doubts began to form in the mind of the Director of Research. But a lot of time had been spent already with the candidates. They had been wined and dined, met staff, and some of the Institute's VIPs had given them both the seal of approval. The Director could not say for sure why he was uncertain, but there was something about both of them that made the Director believe that neither would be able to do the job. But at this stage, not appointing one of them would reflect badly on him.

Going back and starting again could be seen as failure. It would be his fault that the perfect candidate had not applied the first time round. No one would believe that for some other reason the right person, who must be out there, had not applied.

But the work of the laboratory was getting behind and staff were getting increasingly concerned about the delay. The pressure was on to make an appointment. A voice inside kept telling him that, in these circumstances, the worst thing he could do would be to appoint someone who could not do the job. Another two months delay would be far worse than having to sort out a poor appointment. Or would it?

Getting behind the words

During an interview, events move fast. There are a number of questions to be asked and topics to be discussed. The interviewers each have points to raise, and the candidates have questions. There is little time to think during the exchange and the next candidate is due in immediately afterwards. It is virtually impossible to call a candidate back into the room to ask them to explain what was meant by a particular answer if on reflection there is doubt in the interviewers' minds. Yet sometimes there is need for clarification and probing.

We all want people to succeed and do their best. Generally we tend to look for the good in people. Some people are so desperate for a job that they go to any lengths to secure one. Candidates fabricate CVs and find obliging others to provide references or testimonials. Qualifications are invented and employment records created. An interviewer needs to be prepared for people not telling the whole truth. Some may avoid the question, others may slant the question so they are able to provide the answer they want to give, others may lie.

To deal with this sort of situation, interviewers need to be:

❑ ready to think quickly
❑ prepared to go back to a topic and ask the unresolved question again in a slightly different way
❑ prepared to doubt and probe until the reservations are resolved one way or another
❑ ready to ask the candidate to provide factual evidence such as dates of projects, length of time to complete an assignment, amount of money generated by a campaign, etc.

Another aspect of a candidate's behaviour in interviews which may mislead interviewers is due to gender difference. Some men, it has been found, tend to claim successes, even if they were achieved by team effort. Some women tend to deny their contribution and, even when success was their responsibility, they give credit to others or ascribe it to luck. Similarly, some men attribute failure to bad luck, and some women blame themselves for being inadequate. Some men approach a new job confident in their abilities to carry out all the duties competently from the very beginning. Some women tend to be less sure of themselves, cautious about their abilities and conscious of their development needs. These tendencies will influence how a candidate presents him or herself.

Interviewers need to be aware of this and be ready to explore in depth with the candidates. In practice this means:

❑ choosing the questions and topics for discussion carefully
❑ listening carefully to the words given in reply
❑ thinking about what may be behind what people say
❑ avoiding attributing motivations and guessing why a candidate has behaved or replied in certain ways

❑ probing by asking the candidate to say more and explain for themselves
❑ watching how candidates react
❑ having the support of another interviewer to follow up a question and get behind superficial answers.

Effect of group dynamics on decision making

An interview panel works like any other group of people and is equally prone to the positive and negative effects of group dynamics. Groups can make better-quality decisions than individuals alone as they allow a range of perspectives, experiences and views to be considered. They also enable group members to test out their opinions and check with each other that their beliefs about the candidates and the evidence on which those beliefs have been based are sound. They also provide the ground for other issues to be played out. This can result in conflict and power play.

Example 41

All the doctors knew that Marguerite was due to retire, but when the day came the partners realised just how badly prepared they were. The advertisement to fill her role as Practice Manager had been placed weeks before and the interviews were set up. But Marguerite had been the stalwart of the practice. She had been there since there was just one GP, and had been instrumental in its growth into its present form, now the largest fundholding practice in town, and had established all the systems and procedures. In effect she *was* the Green Health Centre.

The GPs were equal partners in the practice and had regular monthly meetings at which decisions were taken on the basis of consensus. They had discussed the mechanics of filling Marguerite's post but not the implications of her retirement. It was almost as if another Marguerite would appear and everything would carry on as before. But not all the doctors saw it like that, or even wanted it. Two of the younger doctors had discussed how the retirement would create the opportunity

Continued on next page

Continued from previous page

for change. Some of the old-fashioned ways could go and, by investing in new technology, a massive sea change could be brought about. What was needed to replace Marguerite was a new broom.

Another partner had given the matter absolutely no thought. She just wanted a quite life, someone to make sure everything ticked over. The two senior partners were quite clear. It was obvious; no discussion was needed. A new Marguerite would replace the old Marguerite. Nothing would change.

Six applicants were invited to the Health Centre, to meet the partners and attend an interview. After the interviews the doctors made up their minds about whom to appoint. Appointing five practice managers was not an option. The meeting following the interviews lasted five hours and blew apart any semblance of consensual decision making. The schisms in the practice came into the open and the need to replace Marguerite provided the arena for many of the previously unspoken tensions to be aired.

❏ One of the junior partners wanted to appoint a man to introduce the sort of changes needed to move from 'housekeeping', as he called it, into 'business practice'.
❏ The other accused him of being sexist, only concerned with systems; a mere technie who had no idea about people management and the humanity needed for the provision of a quality service.
❏ The third could not see what all the fuss was about. Any one of the candidates would do so long as they made sure that the patients and their notes appear together.
❏ The founder GP was furious! Why change anything? The practice had done very nicely under Marguerite's type of management and organisation. One of the applicants would be a superb replacement. She had exactly the same approach.
❏ His supporter was less convinced about the need to remain totally unchanged. The record system was groaning. Something had to happen. There had been too many incidents of lost case notes recently.

If only they had discussed it before placing the advertisement.

Groups can avoid the negative impact of internal dynamics and work effectively towards a decision by having an agreed process and preferably one agreed individual who is responsible for leading the group. Even in consensus decision making someone is needed to steer the group. Therefore, the role of the main interviewer is to make sure that all interviewers:

❑ are aware of the criteria for appointment
❑ understand what these criteria mean in practice
❑ know and comply with their role
❑ agree to the decision-making process
❑ follow the agreed process.

She or he is also responsible for spotting when extraneous matters are being brought in and taking steps to minimise their impact.

Stress of process

Another influence on interviewers is stress. We have already noted the importance of an appointment decision and the possibly damaging consequences of a wrong appointment. Being an interviewer is a responsible job which can be stressful. Not only is the importance of the occasion a source of stress; sometimes the need to make an appointment can be a source of pressure. Decision making under pressure can be dangerous as it can make interviewers feel obliged to appoint. They have to make a decision, any decision, rather than no decision, for, as we have seen above, sometimes the decision not to appoint can be seen as not being an option.

Making rushed decisions can be risky. It is important, therefore, not to build an interview timescale that is too onerous. Stress and tiredness together lead to mistakes. Interviewers should be allowed to concentrate only on the job of interviewing: doing too many tasks at once overloads the brain, and overloaded brains do not search fully for information and do not consider all options. They go for the easiest mental route and the most readily available piece of data. Tired brains do not check their perceptions or the accuracy of the information they are using. They make snap decisions and then resist any pressure to change them. This sort of decision making in interviewing can lead to disasters.

Example 42

Filling the post of Production Manager was vital for the company's survival. Jim's untimely death had been a real tragedy for everyone, not just his family. He had been a visionary and always knew what to do in a crisis. The latest was as unexpected as his car crash. A major customer had gone bust owing the company several thousands of pounds and the process control system had developed gremlins. Even though there was scope to recoup the loss and find new customers, the company could not produce the goods. Someone was urgently needed to sort out the production process control system.

Head hunters had hunted, adverts had been placed, candidates met, wined and interviewed. But no one seemed to up to the mark. The MD swore that the next person through the door with a degree in process control engineering would get the job. Someone was better than no one!

No matter how much pressure is on to make an appointment, it has to be the right person. The result of getting it wrong would be even more terrible.

Expectations and the influence of others outside the process

Sometimes pressure to appoint a particular candidate, regardless of who is the best, comes from outside the process and people directly involved.

Example 43

Alexis knew she should let Peter make the appointment. It would be his first since his promotion, but she could not resist. She read through the application letters and was delighted to see that one was from a previous employee. 'Wouldn't it be splendid to have Jonas back', she said to Peter. Jonas duly appeared on the interview list. Immediately after his interview, Alexis rushed in. 'How was he?', she asked. 'Will you be able to appoint him? Oh, I mustn't interfere. You must make your own decision, Peter.' But how much real freedom did Peter have?

DECIDING WHOM TO APPOINT

Even when the criteria are explicit, agreed and clear, a mechanism to aid decision making can improve the process. Normally after any type of interview, the interviewers will meet together to decide whom to appoint. Some means of combining their observations and agreeing which candidate best matches the sought-for criteria, is most likely to perform the job to the required standard and will best fit the organisation's culture, is desirable. There are several steps to take.

Discounting unsuitable candidates

Eliminating candidates should be founded on demonstrable evidence that can be fed back to the individual, should they request it. Simply rejecting a person because the interviewers did not like them, or because they simply 'did not perform on the day' is neither good enough, nor legal.

The following way of deciding which of the candidates are not appointable because they do not meet the standard also reduces the negative effects of group dynamics.

The interviewers write down the name(s) of any candidate(s) who do not meet any of the criteria. This is done before any discussion, thus removing the possibility of one interviewer's opinion influencing the others.

If there is a consensus on any name(s), those are eliminated.

Consideration of their performance comes after the remaining candidates have been assessed. This focuses the interviewers' attention on the candidates who are appointable.

Candidates who have been eliminated are discussed after it has been decided who to appoint so that they can be given feedback if asked, and to comply with record-keeping procedures, such as equal opportunities monitoring.

The remaining candidates are assessed in turn, detailed examination of the evidence carried out and a decision regarding who best meets the criteria reached.

Pooling the evidence

A simple matrix can help interviewers combine the evidence they have collected about the candidates during the course of the interviews. From the example given on pages 41–43 for the trainee accountant, here is a matrix drawn from the person specification.

Example 44

	EVIDENCE				
SOURCE	Application	Group 1	Group 2	Reference	Interview
CRITERIA					
Computer literate					
Compilation of accurate financial reports					
Preparation of concise and clearly written reports					
Able to give clear verbal presentations					
Influencing skills					
Problem analysis and solving					
Interpersonal and team-working skills					

Evidence is collected against each of the criteria from different sources. Using Example 44:

❏ The application form or letter would have been analysed, and the main interviewer from Group 1 and 2 would have prepared a report assessing the candidate's behaviour and responses.
❏ The references, if any had been obtained, would be checked for collaborating evidence.
❏ The final interview would be conducted to fill any gaps and make sure that all the criteria had been adequately explored.
❏ At the end of the whole process a matrix would be completed for each candidate. Short notes would be made, providing examples of when and how the candidates demonstrated their abilities against each of the criteria.
❏ Finally, comparison would be made between the candidates.

The matrix also acts as a record and can be used if there is any need, later, to demonstrate the fairness and equity of the decision.

Scoring

A matrix can be made more sophisticated by incorporating a scoring mechanism.

✓   the skill or required knowledge was found
✗   the skill or knowledge was not demonstrated
0   no evidence was found (neutral)
?   further exploration is required

Another way is to give a specific score, for example using a behavioural anchored-rating scale:

Example 45

Concern for Quality
Ability to take action to maintain and improve the quality of service and 'customer' satisfaction.

Definition	Rating
Quality issues are not recognised	1
Knows that quality is important but does not know what to do about it	2
Can maintain quality and customer satisfaction but does not know how to achieve it	3
Recognises some areas where actions can be taken to make improvements	4
Has general ideas about how to improve quality services and customer satisfaction but does not translate them into practice	5
Develops and implements ways for maintaining and improving quality services and customer satisfaction	6

Or a simple, absolute scale, as shown in Example 45.

Example 46

Rating Scale

Definition	Rating
Use of the skill was not evident	1
The skill was used to limited effect	2
The skill had a slight impact – much improvement is needed	3
The skill was used to some effect, but there is room for improvement	4
The skill was effective most of the time; some refinement is possible	5
The skill was used to full effect	6

The numbers would be used in the matrix to represent the definitions instead of words describing the evidence. The interviewers need to share the same understanding of the definitions' meaning and how numbers are being used in the matrix.

It is possible to ascribe a weighting to the criteria if so desired. If, for example, the Trainee Accountant's ability to give verbal presentations was critical, this skill would be weighted at 5, influencing skills the second most important, at 4, problem solving next at 3, and so on. These weightings would be used as multipliers in the matrix and added up to give an overall score. The final scores would then be used to order the candidates, and the one with the highest result would be the preferred candidate. Before any decision to appoint is made, the interviewers would need to compare their assessment of the candidates' abilities and predicted potential to do the job. Any difference would be explored to discover the reason for the mismatch. This exploration would enable the interviewers' to check the accuracy and foundation of their assessments, make sure that number crunching was not taking over from judgement and, only then, arrive at a decision that could be justified and evidenced.

Consensus

Obtaining consensus is by far the best way to decide who is the best candidate. This can be obtained by taking each of the candidates in turn and asking each of the interviewers to assess them by asking, 'Could this person perform the job, as defined, to the standard required?' Each of the criteria is assessed and a conclusion reached about the candidate's overall potential to do the job. If the answer is 'No', the reasons for this are elicited from the interviewers, recorded and used as a record and for feedback.

After all the candidates have been considered, those remaining are examined again, against these criteria:

❑ who will do the best job
❑ who will best meet the organisational requirements
❑ who will be the best social fit
❑ who has the most future potential.

Only then if there is clearly no one best candidate, need they be compared one against another.

This rational decision making allows each interviewer to make a full contribution. Thus they will feel able to own the outcome. The procedure can also reduce some of the negative effects of group dynamics. It will lead to a decision that can be communicated outside as it will be defensible should it be challenged at a later date.

If there is no clear outcome, you have to find some other means of reaching a decision. Some of the other rational decision-making methods, such as decision trees or decision analysis, could be used. They tend to deny the importance of interpersonal exchanges and the assessment of social fit and can leave the interviewers with a sense of being overtaken by the method. Consequently if consensus is not possible, all that remains is some form of voting.

Voting

This is the most common way of making a group decision when unanimity is not possible. A straight show of hands and a clear majority may produce a favoured candidate, but if the decision is not that clear cut, some more elaborate way of choosing the best candidate needs to be found. There are sophisticated forms of voting, such as transferable votes, that can be used, but when appointing people to do jobs greater care than that is needed.

Consideration also needs to be given to the consequences of dissent:

❑ What will happen to the interviewers who do not agree with the end decision and are left with the feeling of being outvoted?
❑ How are they going to behave towards the appointee once they are in post?
❑ How will the voting process withstand scrutiny, if one of the candidates believes that they have been unfairly treated?

The chair of the interview panel will need to ensure that:

❏ the decision is made on the basis of evidence
❏ the criteria used for the voting are those that have been used throughout the process
❏ each candidate was judged fairly on their ability to perform the job to the required standard.

HOW TO AVOID THE PITFALLS

Training interviewers, it has been said, achieves no change in behaviour, but simply makes them more aware of what they are doing wrong. In fact this increased awareness can be a major step forward, if we take these four steps as a measure of learning:

❏ unconscious incompetence
❏ conscious incompetence
❏ conscious competence
❏ unconscious competence.

SUMMARY

Interviewers should be aware of the pitfalls and dangers of making their judgements too early.

1. *First impressions can be flawed and there is no shame in admitting that, during the early stages of an interview, the information is not adequate to allow proper assessments to be made.* Appearance, initial behaviour, language, culture, and motivation alone, are not adequate predicators of subsequent performance in the job.

   An interviewer's memory is not a reliable source of information. The memory store uses hooks to ease recall, and candidates seen first and last are·more likely to be remembered. Similarly, the individual who has an outstanding feature or who does something out of the ordinary, is likely to stick out from the rest. Other means of being able to remember each candidate as a distinct individual are required.

2. *Notes, memory aids, sketches and so on will help you recall the candidate, and will contribute to the needed records of the interview.* We all like to be surrounded by people we like, so are subconsciously attracted to people who share similar characteristics, backgrounds and values. We use our own rules of thumb, which have been built up over our lifetime, to do this. As they are based on history, they work most of the time, but not always.

3. *Be aware of the factors that influence how you assess other people on first meetings.* The candidate is seen as being centre of the stage, every stage. Interviewers tend to believe that they have had a major effect on the events that have happened around them. This could reflect well or badly on the candidates, when in reality they were minor players or not even on the stage at all when the event occurred.

4. *Check, directly with the candidate, the extent of their role and contribution.* If the first impression has been used as the foundation for assessment, interviewers tend to seek confirmation of this view and actively discount contradictory evidence. This can be dangerous, as many managers, who subsequently have performance problems with staff, find out. The indicators of the problem were seen but, for one reason or another, ignored during the interview.

5. *Doubt your own judgement and test out your perceptions with other interviewers. Obtaining other sources of evidence, for example from a case study, work sample, or behavioural event interview, is also recommended.* Other people's views can be unreliable. The reasons for their opinion can be totally unrelated to the candidate's ability to perform the job for which they are applying in your organisation. Even though there is a duty of care on referees to be accurate in what they say, there is still a tendency to wrap up references in bland generalities.

6. *Use reference checks for matters of fact and rely only on people, whose views are valid and in context, to express opinions about the candidates' abilities to perform to the standard required.* Some candidates do their best to sell themselves and interviewers, ready to see the good in

people, want them to succeed. There are occasions when candidates tell lies or half truths in their efforts to convince interviewers they are the best candidate. Some research has demonstrated that men and women adopt different approaches to presenting themselves in interviews. There can also be differences due to cultural expectations.

7. *Escalating one's investment in a decision can be simply a further waste of resources. It may be better to cut your losses if the candidates do not match the requirements, and start again, rather than appoint someone who does not meet the minimum criteria.* Once the interview process is well under way, interviewers feel some pressure to continue, even when it looks as though the best outcome would be not to make an appointment.

8. *Probe and get behind the words spoken to find real evidence of ability and achievement.* Group dynamics can influence the interviews by allowing issues unconnected with the appointment to be introduced.

9. *The chair of the interview panel is responsible for taking a lead and ensuring that the other interviewers focus on the job in hand and the criteria being sought.* The chair is also responsible for making sure the other interviewers are able to perform their role in the process. Interviewing is stressful and tiring. Interviewers are under pressure to make the right appointment yet are often fully aware of the importance of what they are doing. Additionally, pressure can be applied by others not directly involved.

10. *The chair of the panel needs to make sure that all concerned are aware of pressure, that appropriate allowances are made and undue external pressure is resisted.* After the interviews are completed, some mechanism is needed to ensure that decisions are taken on the basis of examination of the evidence collected against the criteria being sought. This includes:

❏ discounting unsuitable candidates
❏ pooling the evidence
❏ using an appropriate rating or scoring system

❑ reaching consensus, whenever possible
❑ voting as a last resort.

Even though the decision has been made, the process is not yet over. A verbal contract may have been made, but the detailed negotiations of the terms and conditions of the appointment have to be finalised. Unsuccessful candidates deserve feedback and the person to be appointed will have early development needs. Induction and steps to ensure the new starter is properly included into their new job and organisation need to be taken. Ways of taking these important steps are outlined in the next chapter.

6

AFTER THE INTERVIEW

The interview does not stop when the last candidate has walked out of the door and the interviewers have decided who was the best. There is more work to be done. Some of this will be pleasant for the interviewers, some less so. Some of the tasks may have legal implications and all of them will have some impact on the candidates. People applying for a job are doing more than selling themselves as a product; they invest time, dreams, and a great deal of personal information with a prospective employer. How that organisation deals with them after the interview process will have an impact on their view of the organisation as an employer. This view may be positive but, if the interviewers do not handle the post-interview exchanges well, the unsuccessful candidates may be left feeling bruised and unimpressed. Even the person appointed to the post can be left to wonder why they want to work there, unless some simple steps are taken to consolidate the interview process to an outcome that has benefits for all parties.

MAKING THE OFFER

Once the interviewers have decided which candidate best matches the criteria, the chosen individual is asked if he or she is prepared to accept the job. There are several ways in which the offer of employment can be made.

1. All the candidates can be asked to wait until all the interviews have been completed. Alternatively, they can be asked to return at a given time. This is only really feasible when a

few individuals have been interviewed, if there is suitable waiting space for them and/or the candidates can be occupied in a suitable way.

2. The selected candidate can be contacted by telephone later that day or in the days immediately following. This is probably the most commonly used means of making an offer. It is fast, it enables a discussion to take place and the interviewer to gauge whether the individual is likely to accept.

3. The selected candidate can be sent a letter making an offer of employment. This is slower (fax can be used to speed it up) but ensures that the terms and conditions of employment are clearly set out.

Whatever method is used to convey the offer, the candidate makes the final decision. They have the power to accept or reject the offer. In practical terms, not many candidates refuse an offer of employment, but there is always the possibility that they choose not to enter into a legally binding agreement. If the offer is accepted, terms and conditions of employment should be spelt out and agreed before the contract is finalised. This contract need not be written (employees do not have the legal right to such a document) and need not be signed. The candidate turning up for work on the first day is enough to enable an employer to assume the contract has been accepted.

Nevertheless, under the Trade Union Reform and Employment Rights Act (1994) all employers are entitled to receive a written statement of terms and conditions. Agreeing these is important before a formal contract is exchanged. For most jobs these explicit terms are straightforward but it is worth taking a little care clarifying the implicit terms. The implicit terms of a contract are not written as they relate to expectations and cultural assumptions such as standards, working practice, and relationships. If these are not made clear at the beginning of a period of employment misunderstandings, under-performance and, possibly, ultimate failure can result. Consequently, investing a little more time by treating the period between the making of the offer of employment and formal acceptance as one of negotiation can be beneficial in the longer term.

This approach tends to be adopted for senior appointments. It is not unusual for further meetings and discussions to be held between the individual and new employer. If recruitment consultants have been employed, they can be used to advise on or even negotiate the package and any 'transfer' arrangements. Even if this sounds like football, the complexities of some senior manager's contracts merit the same sort of careful discussion and, perhaps, for documents to be legally drawn up. If this seems unduly formal, consider the size of some of the settlements made and difficulties encountered when contracts of employment, even at less senior levels, are terminated early. No one likes to start a new relationship by considering its termination, but failure to take care of the details at the opening stage can lead to high legal fees at its end.

Example 47

Mary was offered the job of career grade administrator. During the interview she had checked her understanding of the career grade's operation as the advertisement had not been very clear. She was told that her salary would progress incrementally each year until she reached the sixth and maximum point of the grade.

After two years in post, Mary was surprised when she did not receive the expected increment. She was told she had reached the bar and would not progress until there was more responsibility for her to take on. Somewhat aggrieved, Mary complained to a tribunal who agreed that her contract did not provide for a salary bar and instructed her employer to honour the (verbal) contract.

Even though the wording of an offer of employment needs care, it is usually a happy occasion, when success and new beginnings can be celebrated. It also provides additional opportunities. It is rare, in the glow of the outcome, to consider the successful candidate's weak points. The person selected is seen as being capable of good all-round performance. It is expected that after the first day they will be used to finding their way round, they will 'hit the ground running'. This expectation is both unreasonable and unfair.

The interview provides for an almost uniquely detailed assessment of an individual's abilities against pre-determined criteria. A profile of the successful candidate's strengths and weaknesses can be compiled against those criteria. This profile provides valuable information to be fed back to the candidate and can be used to devise initial training and a subsequent development plan.

INFORMING UNSUCCESSFUL CANDIDATES

Telling unsuccessful candidates that they will not be offered the post requires care and sensitivity. Giving people bad news is never easy and there is no perfect solution to help the interviewer to get it right. There are several options:

❑ The content of the message can be short and to the point ('sorry, you are not being offered the post').
❑ It can be wrapped in platitudes ('you were all very strong candidates; we had a very difficult time in choosing between you; we were very impressed with your track records').
❑ It can leave candidates unsure about what is happening ('we need to have further discussions, consider further options, be in touch next week').

The last option is not satisfactory from anyone's point of view, even though it does happen. If this approach is used, candidates will be left with the impression of prevarication and indecision. The second option, regrettably, is common. Candidates can have mixed feelings and be confused – elated by having done well, and disappointed by failure.

Clearly the first option is preferable. Candidates should be left wanting to apply again for another post, not thankful of having had a lucky escape. This means that the message should be clear, informative and aimed at helping the candidates improve on their applications and interviewing practice.

To achieve this consider how you will convey the message,

before the content is decided. If the candidates have been asked to wait, the candidate to whom the offer is to be made has to be separated from the others.

Example 48

Two interviewers joined the waiting candidates in a meeting room. One asked the person to be offered the job to leave the room with them, while the chair of the interview panel thanked the remaining candidates for their application and attending the interview. They were informed that their application has not been successful, that their application (not the person) did not match the job requirements and that, if they wished, personal feedback would be available later. If they wanted to take up that offer they could either telephone the chair or make a personal appointment.

If the candidates have not waited until the end of the interviews, you can let them know the decision by asking them to return to the premises, arranging to telephone them, or by sending a letter. The first option means that the message can be given personally and feedback be made available 'on the spot', if wanted. The telephone makes the message less personal but still allows some discussion and the option of feedback. The third option is the most impersonal and provides no immediate opportunity for dialogue.

Some may argue that dialogue is not desirable as the more information given to unsuccessful candidates, the more evidence they have available should they wish to complain. This view does not provide any help for the candidates nor does it repay the effort the candidates have made in submitting the application. They deserve something more from the process than just experience, the opportunity to meet some new people, and rejection. In saying this, it has to be recognised that some candidates may feel so aggrieved that they will grasp the opportunity to find cause for complaint. Consequently consideration needs to be given to how much and what kind of information should be given to unsuccessful candidates.

Generally, candidates can be told:

❏ they have not been appointed
❏ the name of the person who has been offered the post
❏ whether the offer has been accepted, is still being considered or has been refused
❏ in the case of the latter, what is to happen next (for example, reconsider the post, re-advertise, re-examine all the applications).

Candidates should not be told:

❏ why the individual offered the post was chosen
❏ they were the second choice
❏ they were unsuccessful the first time round but will be considered again
❏ they were not good enough.

If there is reason to doubt the chosen candidate's acceptance, it might better to wait before informing the other candidates that their application has not been successful. If the person chosen initially turns down the job, offering the job to a candidate who did not meet the criteria during the first interview can be inadvisable.

Telling candidates that they were not good enough can be insulting, hurtful and provide motives for complaint. Do not reject the *person*. It is better to make it clear that the match between the individual's skills, knowledge, experience, approach and the organisation's required criteria was not close enough.

Providing too much information is as dangerous as giving too little or the wrong sort. Interviewers do not have to justify why a candidate has not been offered a post. All that is needed is to state the candidate did not match the criteria. Candidates can be offered personal feedback at a later time, if they want. This puts the onus on the individual to seek feedback and more information at a time of their choosing, when they are psychologically prepared to receive it. Just after being told that they are not being offered a wanted job is not necessarily the best time. If nothing else, it is likely the candidates will feel disappointed, hurt or even angry. They may not be able to take in what is being said. They may be experiencing some negative feelings about themselves, the interview, the interviewers and the organisation. Delaying the giving of feedback also gives the interviewers the time to put the message into a more constructive form and to prepare practical suggestions designed to help the candidates improve their performance, fill gaps in their experience, knowledge or skill levels, and learn from the experience.

If a candidate feels unfairly treated and believes he or she has a justifiable cause for grievance, the right exists to complain to an industrial tribunal. For this to happen the individual needs to believe that he or she has been discriminated against unlawfully (on the grounds of gender, race, religion, marital status, or disability). If the decision regarding the best candidate has been made rigorously by assessing each person's competence to carry out the duties to the standard required and fit against a set of predetermined criteria, employers should be able to defend their action.

GIVING FEEDBACK

Feedback should not be imposed on unsuccessful candidates. They should be offered the opportunity to receive it, at a time and in a way with which they are comfortable. There are some very simple guidelines, which provide the opportunity for both the giver and recipient to learn and identify ways of improving on practice.

❏ The person to give the feedback should be the one who was responsible for the appointment. It is not a job to be left to the human resource department.
❏ The candidate should be encouraged to reflect on their own performance.
❏ If the criteria have been made public, remind the candidate of these.
❏ Ask the candidate to consider, for themselves, why they were not offered the post, in the context of the criteria. This gives the candidate the opportunity to say what they think about the process and, if aggrieved in any way, they are able to state their position.

❑ If the candidate expresses any concerns, these should be addressed before any attempt is made to give feedback for, if they are angry or upset, information will not be properly heard or may cause further aggravation.

Once the ground has been properly set, feedback can be given to the candidate. Use, as a starting point, the candidate's own perception of their performance. Usually candidates have a feeling for where they did not match the criteria but, sometimes, they need a framework and someone else to help them articulate it. A skilled interviewer can often elicit enough feedback from the candidate by acting as a 'looking glass', without having to add information. This approach can be particularly useful if the candidate is angry or emotional.

When the candidate is ready to receive information, the following summarises good practice:

❑ *Keep the reason for providing the feedback clearly in view.* Its purpose is to help the candidate move forward, not to tell them where they failed.
❑ *Judge the amount of detail to provide.* If too much detail is given, the candidate will not be able to absorb it all, and may feel overloaded and unable to cope with what is being said. It is better to move gradually from general pointers, testing how much information the individual is able to accept, before moving to detailed specifics.
❑ *Focus on behaviour that can be changed.*
❑ *Provide evidence of the behaviour to be changed* by referencing what the candidate did or said during the interview and offer examples of alternative approaches. Make it clear these are just indicators, not specific incidents to be taken out of context.
❑ *Suggest ways in which improvements could be achieved.*
❑ *The evidence presented should be factually accurate and demonstrable.*
❑ *Avoid passing judgement.* The use of adjectives, such as poor, good, or better, invite the candidate to ask for examples of alternatives, which can be difficult to give. What may be good in one context could be awful in another.
❑ *Make use of positives.* Candidates should be told they have

strengths as well as shortcomings. It is likely that a poor candidate for one job will be the best for another.

❏ *Candidates have the right not to accept the feedback.* They may not wish to accept the feedback or act on the suggestions for change.

❏ *Do not leave the candidate with no sense of the future.* No one is totally unemployable.

Example 49

During the interview, Matthew, you said that the job needed someone who was able to control production by setting tight quality standards and volume targets. In fact, while we recognise the value of this approach, we are looking for someone who would encourage the workers to take responsibility for controlling the quality and quantity of their own output. Perhaps it would help you if you were to talk to some managers who had experience of working in this way.

CONFIDENTIALITY

During an interview and as part of their application for a job, candidates make available large quantities of personal information. Their backgrounds are described in detail, they are encouraged to engage in analysis of their skill levels, outline the extent of their knowledge and give out personal facts about their earlier lives. They are asked to consider their futures and tell probably unknown interviewers where they see themselves going for the rest of their careers. Information about the candidates is obtained from third parties and assessment notes are made describing the interviewers' observations and judgements. Records are made and files are kept.

How often, as appointers, do we consider the confidentiality of all these pieces of information? Photocopies are made of letters of application, application forms and CVs. They are distributed to other interviewers and may be shown to other people. What happens to these extra copies? Are these shredded after the interview, filed in someone's desk or placed carefully and completely into the waste-paper basket? The top copies of the paper-work relating to the person appointed are needed to begin a personal file, but what happens to the unsuccessful candidates' files?

Some of the information gathered is not only recorded on paper; some remains in the interviewers' memories. What is said by candidates and others inside and out of the formal process to interviewers also deserves to be treated with confidence.

Example 50

Phillippa had had enough. She was fed up with being put down. She knew her market research was as good as the others in the team, yet she was constantly denied opportunities to attend professional meetings. Her boss tried to belittle her in front of her colleagues and laughed with them about her efforts. She decided it was time to move.

When a similar job became vacant in one of her employer's major competitors she submitted her application and was pleased to be invited for an interview. During the interview she was asked many probing questions, about her work and, to her surprise, about that of her colleagues. She tried to be helpful and appear open while not giving away anything that might be construed as a trade secret: not easy when trying to impress a potential employee.

Phillippa was distressed to learn that she had not been appointed and was concerned when she learnt that the post had been offered to someone whose experience was very different from her own. She wondered why she had been interviewed at all. After a few months the answer became clear. The competing company started to work in exactly the same areas as her current employer. It appeared she had been interviewed purely so that the competitor could pump her for inside information.

Who, if anyone, had acted unethically in Example 50? Similar horror stories abound. Interviewers, after a long day of interviews, have been heard laughing and joking in public places about candidates. This may be a release of stress, but is it proper, professional behaviour? Candidates deserve to be treated with respect so everything that happens in the interview room should remain in confidence. In that way everyone is safeguarded, no secrets are betrayed and no one will have grounds to accuse the interviewers of improper treatment, malpractice or unethical behaviour.

RECORDS

Proper records should be made at the time of interviews and maintained for a period afterwards. If an individual believes he or she has been subjected to illegal discrimination and treated unfairly, the right to complain to an industrial tribunal exists. These rights are laid down in the sex discrimination, race relations and other anti-discriminatory legislation. If a case is raised, the tribunal will require the papers to be made available for examination and cross-examination. At one time, there was a laid-down timescale after which an aggrieved individual was debarred from submitting a complaint. This has now been removed. The implication is that records of interviewers and other selection activities need to be maintained for a longer period. This need should be considered when designing the supporting systems and forms. The records need not be lengthy. Rather, they should be concise, factual, readable, understandable by a third party and contain:

❑ the job description, person specification and any other selection criteria identified
❑ the advertisement or other forms of announcement
❑ a brief description of how the shortlisting was carried out or the matrix if used; reasons why an individual was rejected should be briefly and clearly recorded
❑ a record of who was involved in the interview and any other activities used
❑ the assessment results
❑ a list of members of the final interview panel
❑ the formal notes made recording the assessment of each candidate (these should be against the job requirements and criteria)
❑ the reasons for appointment or non-selection.

DEVELOPMENT PLANS

At no other time during employment is an employee assessed in such a detailed way as they are during a selection interview. As a candidate, their history is explored, current skill levels assessed and future potential predicted. The candidate is encouraged to engage in self-reflection, questioning and future planning and the employer makes judgements against specific performance criteria. These assessments can be built into an overall performance management approach which can include the individual's subsequent performance in the job.

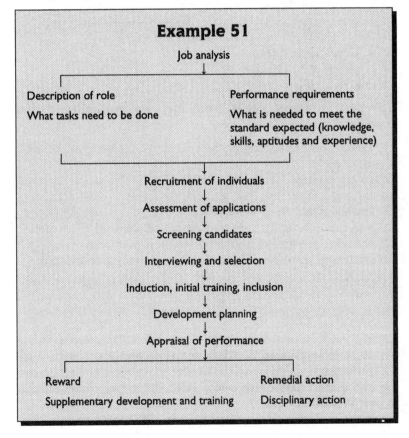

Example 51

Job analysis

Description of role
What tasks need to be done

Performance requirements
What is needed to meet the standard expected (knowledge, skills, aptitudes and experience)

Recruitment of individuals

Assessment of applications

Screening candidates

Interviewing and selection

Induction, initial training, inclusion

Development planning

Appraisal of performance

Reward
Supplementary development and training

Remedial action
Disciplinary action

Induction

Induction provides the information a new staff member needs to help them become an effective member of staff, quickly. Typically, induction begins on the individual's first day at work and should last for the bulk of the first month. Most organisations are not very good at inducting new staff, hence its inclusion as one of the 'Investor's in People' standards. What happens during those first 20 days can have a major influence on the long-term effectiveness of employment. Handled well, the new employee:

❑ settles into the job quickly
❑ learns about the organisation and its culture
❑ builds good-quality working relationships with colleagues
❑ becomes an effective member of staff quickly
❑ achieves agreed targets
❑ contributes to life at work
❑ enjoys their job.

The new employee needs, from the very beginning of their employment:

❑ a clear understanding of the role they are being expected to carry out
❑ an awareness of the standards of performance they are expected to attain
❑ knowledge of their work place
❑ introductions to their immediate colleagues and an awareness of their roles and relationships to their own role
❑ an insight into the culture of the employing organisation.

Many of these can (and should) be covered before the individual actually starts work. There are many opportunities for this to happen, for example:

❑ in the additional information sent out to interested individuals to help them decide whether to apply and focus their application
❑ in the information given to candidates to help them prepare for their interview
❑ in the information supplied as part of the interview process

❑ during the negotiation phase, immediately following the interview
❑ as part of pre-employment visits and discussions.

Initial training

Initial training can only start properly once the individual is in post. However, if the interview assessment is seen as supplying valuable information about the individual's skill and knowledge levels, rather than just applying general training to the individual, a programme can be specially designed to meet their particular needs and be ready to roll as soon as they start work. It can also be tailored to fill in any important gaps in their experience.

Inclusion

Helping the individual fit into the society of the organisation and gain a good understanding of its culture is extremely important to the success of the appointment. Yet this stage of induction is rarely considered. Generally, if steps are taken, they tend to occur as a result of discussions with friendly individuals.

Example 52

The interview had been tough. All the external candidates believed that the job would be offered to the internal candidate, but external candidate, May, worked hard during the interviews; she was really keen. When she was offered the post she was both surprised and delighted. Her first day was a joy: she went home very happy, pleased and looking forward to a satisfying career with her new employer.

It did not take her long to realise that something was wrong. The people around her were remote, and no matter how hard she tried to please her new colleagues, she constantly found herself being shunned. She had not been invited to join the tea club and felt hurt when she discovered that her colleagues went to the pub together on the Friday after pay day. She had not been asked to join them.

Continued on next page

Continued from previous page

This state of affairs continued and made it very difficult for May to do her job. After six months in post, her boss asked to see her and said that he was very disappointed in her. He had hoped that she would settle in quickly and was saddened to hear other staff say she had not made any effort to join in with the team. May decided the best thing she could do was to leave. Fortunately she was able to find another job quickly.

It is easy to see that, in the above example, the cause of the problem lay with the failure to deal with the disappointment of the internal candidate and their supporters. In circumstances such as these, it is important to prepare the way for the new employee immediately following the interview. This is achieved through:

❏ appropriate involvement of staff during the interview process
❏ proper notification of the interviewers' decision to the future colleagues as soon as possible
❏ early meetings with the successful candidate during the course of pre-employment visits.

The employer can also take action to bring the new starter into contact with colleagues in ways that will help their inclusion into the work group. These could include the construction of tasks that require joint working, shadowing, and involvement in projects. They should take account of the formal relationships that need to be established, and the informal and social relationships a new starter will need to build if they are to be a full member of the organisation's wider society.

Some organisations have recognised the importance of inclusion and have developed approaches such as mentoring schemes and 'buddying' to make sure the new starter has an immediate point of contact. These also provide new members of staff with a colleague who will assume responsibility for making sure they have the information they need to carry out their jobs and are assimilated into the organisation quickly.

SUMMARY

Even if the interview has been conducted in text-book fashion, the effect can still be ruined if the post-interview actions are badly done. But if they are considered and handled sensitively, they can leave all the candidates, even those whose applications have not been successful, with a sense of gain.

A staged approach to the offer of employment can lead to a contract of employment whose explicit and implicit terms and conditions are well understood and agreed as they are reached through a phase of negotiation. The inept offer of employment can dissuade the preferred candidate from accepting the job.

Unsuccessful candidates at the very least deserve the offer of feedback. They should be allowed to decide if they want to accept the offer, and if so, when to receive it. Feedback needs to be given skilfully and with only one purpose in mind – to help the unsuccessful candidates be more successful in their next application and interview.

All candidates deserve to be treated with respect and have the information they provide, in written form or verbally, kept confidential. Surplus paper should be destroyed and spoken comment should not be repeated.

Proper records of the interview need to be kept secure. The papers relating to the appointed candidate form the basis of their personal file. Aggrieved candidates may have the right to complain to an industrial tribunal if they believe they have suffered illegal discrimination. Even if an interviewer is confident they have followed codes of practice and are complying with the law, they must keep records of the interview, the assessments of the candidates and the reasons for appointment or non-appointment.

The assessment of the successful candidate provides valuable and unique information upon which the early training and development plans can be based. Not using this information to link recruitment and selection into other aspects of performance management would be a waste.

Induction is a critical phase of employment. The individual learns about the job, their place in the context of the organisation and its culture. If induction is handled badly, it can sour the whole of the period of employment. If it is got right, perhaps no one will notice as the employee will settle in quickly and easily and soon seem as if they have been in post for ever.

Proper induction also allows the newly appointed individual to be included into the richer life of the organisation. Some schemes such as mentoring and buddying make sure that assimilation is not left to chance.

Appointing staff is far too risky to let any stage rely on chance. Every stage must be carefully planned and fitted together to form a complete process. Decisions are made at various stages and rely totally on the exchange of quality information to enable the parties to make judgements based on evidence rather than impression and assumptions. The interview is the critical point, when the interviewers and the candidates come together formally. Typically the interview lasts no more than one hour: in that time, decisions worth many thousands of pounds are made. The course of an individual's life may be changed and the future of an organisation effected. The time and effort needed to prepare the interview and the interviewers, and plan the overall process, are well spent.

GLOSSARY

Aptitude tests These tests are designed to measure an individual's abilities. Usually the term is applied to mental abilities but tests exist which explore motor skills and manual dexterity. Other areas to be covered include spatial (the ability to relate to shapes), verbal and mechanical reasoning abilities. Some people include cognitive ability tests in this category.

Cognitive ability tests These tests are used to examine an individual's mental or intellectual abilities, such as critical reasoning, numeracy and perceptual skills. Most reputable publishers of psychometric tests supply a range of the most commonly used.

Constructs Abbreviated from 'personal construct theory', a term used by George Kelly to describe the framework of beliefs, experiences, and opinions we develop to help us make sense of our world and to predict likely events or the behaviour of others. Some of these concepts are held so deeply that we are not always aware of holding them.

Criteria This word is used in this book to define aspects of skill, behaviour, knowledge, experience or ability being sought from candidates. They are the fundamental features required for effective performance of the job in question, and, as such, can be learnt. Alternatives include dimensions, features, abilities or aptitudes. The word is not used here to cover personality traits, even though it can be used to do so.

Investors in People This is a government-sponsored scheme designed to stimulate employers' commitment to the training and development of staff. It requires action against four standards – public commitment, the use and communication of a business plan, training staff to help them achieve the plan, and evaluation of the effectiveness of the action taken – if the organisation is to attain the award.

Job analysis The identification of the component parts of the job that needs to be done. This involves collecting information about the tasks, responsibilities and context of the job and may include key relationships and objectives. The results of the analysis are used to form the role outline, job description and person specification and form the basis for a number of human resource management functions. Ways of conducting the analysis are described in Dale and Iles (1992).

Job requirements Used here to describe the criteria and behaviours needed for the particular job in the context of the employing organisation. The same job in a different organisation may have different requirements.

Milk round Similar to a recruitment fair; typically, large employers visit universities and colleges annually, with the intention of recruiting students who will graduate during that year. This can be achieved through providing information, testing and/or interviewing students at the time or inviting them to attend a selection event at a later date.

Psychometric tests A generic term to describe the instruments used to assess an individual's learnt and natural abilities and explore their personality characteristics. The use of these tests has been strongly debated in the personnel and occupational psychology professions and is now subject to a code of conduct issued by the British Psychological Society. The inappropriate and inept use of these tests can cause lasting damage to individuals, therefore they should only be used with care by trained and competent individuals who are as concerned with the ethics of their use and the well-being of the candidates as they are with satisfying the needs of the employer. Most reputable suppliers specify the conditions under which their tests should be used and provide guidelines and material to help with their interpretation.

Whichever test is chosen, the employer should be assured that the test is reliable, has appropriate content and predictive validity.

Schema The organised body of knowledge and experiences used by an individual to interpret their current situation.

Person specification The document that sets out the experience, educational attainments, knowledge, learnt skills and aptitudes required of an individual so that they are able to carry out the duties to the standards required and fulfil the role satisfactorily. Various headings can be used to categorise the requirements.

Speculative letters Individuals, seeking employment, write to employers asking if they have, are likely to have or know of any suitable vacancies. The letters sometimes include a CV or testimonials.

REFERENCES

Bassett, Glenn (1994) 'From job fit to cultural compatibility: evaluating worker skills and temperament in the '90s'. *Journal of Public Sector Management Summer* (11–17)

Cooper, Cary L, and Makin, Peter (1984) *Psychology for professional groups*, BPS and Macmillan Publishers Ltd, London

Dale, Margaret (1995) *Successful recruitment and selection*, Kogan Page, London

Dale, Margaret and Iles, Paul (1992) *Assessing management skills: a guide to competencies and evaluation techniques*, Kogan Page, London

Farr, Robert (1984) 'Interviewing: the social psychology of the interview', in Cooper, C L and Makin, P *op cit.*

Herriot, Peter (1989) *Recruitment in the 90s*, IPM, London

Herriot, Peter (ed.) (1989) *Assessment and selection in organisations: methods and practice for recruitment and appraisal*, Wiley, Chichester

Kelly, George A (1955) *A theory of personality: the psychology of personal constructs*, Norton, New York

Makin, Peter J. (1989) 'Selection of professional groups', in Herriot (ed.) *op cit.*

Smith, Mike, Gregg, M, and Andrews, (1989) *Selection and assessment: a new approach*, Pitman, London

Wicks, Russell P (1984) 'Interviewing: practical aspects', in Cooper, C L and Makin, P *op cit.*

INDEX